dating, mating, and manhandling

Praise for *Dating, Mating and Manhandling*
The Ornithological Guide To Men

"If there were a Nobel Peace Prize in the war between the sexes, Lauren Frances would win it hands down. Read her book and you'll NEVER be lonely again."

– Anne Beatts
Writer, *SNL*

"With her poignant-yet-hilarious book Dating, Mating and Manhandling hot off the presses, Lauren will teach you how to date like an international spy. . . Also on her man-magnet lesson plan: subliminal seduction, body mirroring, and high-octane verbal cues for sure-fire flirting success. Grab your girlfriends and put your fate in your own hands, because the Flirt Fairy's come to town!"

– *Self* magazine

"Men, Lauren Frances has figured us out . . . and our gooses are cooked!"

– Matt Groening
Creator, *The Simpsons*

"With the spunk and wit of Carrie Bradshaw's columns, Frances' rules are for the Sex and the City woman. She's a best friend like Carrie, possesses the street smarts of Samantha when exposing uncomfortable truths, is a total professional like Miranda, and is almost as romantic as Charlotte! She embodies the soul of all four characters and puts the Sex back in the City."

– *Elle* magazine

"She's the flirt fairy!"

– Victoria's Secret

"I've followed every piece of advice Lauren's given me. I suggest you do the same!"

– Amy Brenneman
Amazing Actress, Producer, Activist

"As one of her Romantic Researchers, I can tell you that Lauren's Manhandling techniques are spot-on! She truly has her finger on the pulse of male/female relationships."

– Kate Walsh

"She's saving romance one page at a time!"

– Mark Ruffalo

"Lauren Frances will educate, enlighten, and entertain you. But make no mistake. This woman knows what she is talking about! She'll have you laughing all the way to altar."

– Katherine Woodward Thomas
Author, *Calling in "The One"*

"The women of the world are so fortunate that Lauren Frances has written her brilliant MANifesto! No longer do we need to wonder about anything male–this genius researcher has cracked all of their "code" and made their mysterious, wild ways no longer confusing. She's like a Fairy Godmother and Einstein all rolled into one! And she couldn't be more fun. If you follow her advice, not only will you get to 'happily ever after,' you'll have a rocking good time along the way..."

– Carol Allen
Author, *Love Is in the Stars*

"She's the Doctor of Love, grilling Hollywood one hunk at a time."

– *Extra Weekend Edition*

"Lauren Frances looks like a brunette version of Pamela Anderson and calls herself a Ph. Double D. But behind the title hides itself a counselor, and an authoress who shares the hidden secrets of Mantrapping. This Liebesexpertin coaches Hollywood stars in modern mating behavior, and is the glamorous former life partner of *The Simpsons* creator Matt Groening. She's truly a *"Feminist in a Wonderbra."* We love this book, and you will too!"

– Stern magazine

"With the spunk and wit of Carrie Bradshaw's columns, Frances' rules are for the *Sex and the City* woman. Frances' gals are out on the town, armed with lip gloss and stilettos, flirting and dating (and mating). She takes the classic rules of courtship and applies them to contemporary conundrums. With humorous anecdotes from her "hands on" experience, the book yields effective and empowering advice for woman both in and out of relationships."

– Flaunt magazine

"As an Ornithologist of a special kind, she offers tips for the care and taming of the strangest birds of all: men. She unlocks the flighty and the peacocks and their odd mating rituals. Lauren is a genius at teaching women how to enjoy flirting, get to grips with dating, find their romantic match. She is passionate about what she does, loves her clients and she truly wants to see them find happiness. Lauren Frances, I am glad to report, is the real deal."

– Sunday Independent

"Dating, Mating and Manhandling is filled with the secret keys that conscious, smart woman seeking a lifetime of love must know about to succeed – and that's not even the best part! Through it's pages Lauren Frances will ignite your inner love goddess to give you the authentic confidence (regardless of your age or how long it's been since you dated!) to magnetize the relationship of your dreams. I can't recommend it more highly!"

– Claire Zammit, Ph.D.
Founder, Feminine Power

Lauren Frances

Founder of the Institute for Romantic Research

dating, mating, and manhandling

The Ornithological Guide to Men

Published by Lauren Frances Inc. 2019 All rights reserved.
Illustrations by Konstantine Kakanias

Dating, Mating and Manhandling – An Ornithological Guide to Men was originally published in hardcover by Harmony Books in 2006, an imprint of the Crown Publishing Group, a division of Random House, Inc., New York.

 It was subsequently published as a trade paperback in 2006 by Rizzoli Books, Olympia Publishing, Aufbau Tachenbuch, Kondyli Publishing, and in hardcover by KnophBooks. 2007, 2010 by J& G Gruner + Jahr Polska

Printed as a trade paperback in 2008 and 2019 by Lauren Frances Inc, the2019 edition also includes some revised text in the "Dating" and "Aviary" sections, along with the addition of an author's preface.

I.Title.
HQ801.F684 2006 2005028907
306.73—dc22ISBN-13:978-1-09830-100-2
10987654321

To any woman who's ready for action . . .
and satisfaction!

Hope is the thing with feathers
that perches in the soul
that sings the tune
without the words
and never stops at all.

—Emily Dickinson

Author's Note

Dear Reader,

Every book is like a love story. They're never a sure thing when you begin them, and there's no guarantee that they'll be loved. Writing, like dating, requires a leap of faith, especially when you feel like you're on the wrong side of a Jane Austin novel—and with nary a suitor in tow.

So it's with delight that my field guide to romance has been reprinted in this special edition. Since its original publication, certain references—like flirting in bookstores, or *"wanting to jump into the stockroom with the Italian shoe salesman at Barney's"* —have been rendered obsolete. As such, the text has been edited to be useful for the Romantic Researchers of 2020. But the principles for flirting, dating, and manhandling have proven eternal! And so are its questions.

"Why is it so hard to find someone that I even like, let alone love?" and "Is dating really worth the effort, when I'd much rather be (folding laundry, taking a nap, or spinning flax)?"

So, by way of an answer I thought I'd tell you *this* books story.

After some years of intensive romantic research (practicing the art of flirting, dating, and ahem, mating), I wrote a little field guide to help my sisters in stilettos.

My aim? To help my boy-crazy girlfriends catch the attention of Lovebirds, without chasing them into the hedgerows!

They needed effective Relationship Negotiation Skills, Manhandling Maneuvers, and snappy comebacks to tricky and anxiety-provoking questions like: "Is he marriage-minded or just a Lark?" "How can I keep my thong on—until I'm ready to take it all off?" and how to respond to those three little words, "I need space?"

"What do we say *then!*" my girlfriends cried! My girlfriends wanted *answers*. I thought I'd better give them a cheat-sheet, as they needed this info, and at very odd hours.

Thus, my field notes were hatched and written in my green leather-bound journal with a calligraphy pen. They were reprinted and tucked into dozens of handbags for easy access on numerous date nights by my Romantic Researchers (wing-women), who were on a mission to find worthy, beddable, (and hopefully) marriageable men. And it worked! One by one, we all found love.

I got so inspired, I whipped up my "Romantic Research" into a little book proposal. And like creating a Tinder profile, writing it was fast and fun. But that was the *easy* part. What ensued was more like getting stuck in the first two acts of a very long rom-com.

An offbeat heroine! Literary agent meet-cute! Things looking hopeful! Then . . . stacks of rejection letters. All hopes dashed!

Well, I did what you would do. I shoved this proposal into the back of a drawer, and I moved to Malibu.

Then one summer's day one a deep-cleaning binge, (eight full years later!) I found it right where I'd left it. And as I blew the dust from its pages I thought, "I gotta give this another shot!"

Note: Now if you're feeling dejected about dating (again), or you've been blindsided by a breakup, and your heart's feeling tender and sore . . .

After being rejected, passed over, and abandoned by everyone (including myself), when I gave it another whack, **the exact same book** was . . . adored!

I was suddenly like Amy Schumer in *I Feel Pretty*. Noticed! Quickly courted by five publishing houses, the book became inspired a bidding war, (aka a literary duel). I eloped with Harmony Books in three zippy weeks, and spent months in my turret, writing this book. *What a turnabout!*

And then, some wild events ensued . . .

Everyone suddenly needed a love coach! *Dating, Mating, and Manhandling* was published in hardcover, translated into seven languages, and became an international bestseller. I started sharing my dating and relationship advice on TV shows and in glossy magazines, and *Victoria's Secret* invited me to do a national book signing tour, with my mother as my roadie, in tow.

I started getting adorable nicknames, like *"The Flirt Fairy" "The Man Whisperer"* and *"The Doctor of Love"* on TV. But being called *"Fairy Godmother"* by women from every corner of the globe (can a globe have corners? Why is that a *thing?*)is the dearest thing. Getting invites to Engagements! Weddings! and Baby Showers! (and getting sent pics of The Ring!), really make my heart just sing.

So thirteen years —and countless love stories —later, writing this foreward gave me *vertigo*. What if I'd abandoned this book forever, and hadn't given it one more *go?*

Well, it would have BLEAK, that's what! Like trying to imagine Lizzy-not-winding-up-with-Darcy kind of bleak.

And that's why *Dating, Mating, and Manhandling* is proof that a dash of hopeful expectation, short bursts of effort, and savvy manhandling skills (just borrow mine, it'll save you tons of time*), is definitely the way to go.

Just put a dash of Mantrap Perfume in your décolleté, and slip into your stilettos. 'Cause as the saying goes, after all, *"Who knows?"*

All my love & *"Onward Ho!"*

Lauren Frances

Los Angeles
January 2020

* Please feel free to send me your "reports from the field" to www.laurenfrances.com! I love getting your emails, and read every single one!

Acknowledgments

My heartfelt thanks to the following, for taking me under your wing!

To Everyone at Fabfitfun! I send you overflowing buckets of Orange Blossom love! Thank you for asking for this special edition of *Dating, Mating and Manhandling*, and for giving Lovescript, *Bath, Beauty and Boudoir* the most spectacularly supportive perch! A special thanks to Lyndsay Patterson, Chelsey Klemm, and Lynda Phan, for being human sparkle powder!

To *My Soul Sistahs*: Amy Brenneman, you never cease to amaze, with your gorgeous gossamer wings. And our beloved Soul Sistah's: Alexa Jung, Annie Potts, Susan McMartin, Jessica Tuck, Donna Mastropasqua, Nancy Neufeld, Lucinda Jenney, and Ishtar!, our friendship is a wonderful thing. To my sisters-from-another-mother: Carol Allen, Nina Meladandri & Marilee Albert, the joy to my llife. you bring! And to my Fairy Goddaughter Sarah Blakley-Cartwright, your pointed edits are perfection.

To my readers and *Romantic Researchers in the field, Man Magnets, seminar graduates, podcast listeners, and private coaching clients:* Thank you for believing in love! Allowing me to support your dreams and seeing them become your reality. is not just a total blast. It's an honor!

To my *Lovescript Dream Team*: Andy Gilbert, Laura Nowatzki-Bilek, Meiyume and the whole Berlin family! Thank you for making my inventive dreams come true. We're making magic! And a special thanks to Salah Ahmed for burning the midnight oil, with me. We did it!!

To my beloved mother Barbara: Thank you for being an irrepressible flirt, and for teaching me the secret to meaningfully living - with your arms flung wide open, and joyously giving!

And last but not least . . .

. . . to my blonde dog Penelope, the best writing buddy ever! Thank you for being the most fetching companion imaginable, in your darling pink cable knit sweater!

Contents

part iii: manhandling

Introduction

It has often been said that men are dogs. Any dog owner will be quick to point out the obvious flaw in this unfair comparison. Although men do indeed sometimes behave like "dirty dogs", this refers to their mutual love of recreational sex and their willingness to engage in it anywhere, anytime — and even in the middle of the road.

But sadly, the analogy stops there.

Dogs are *remarkably* easy to train. This is clearly not true of most men. Trying to get them to put down a toilet seat can take a lifetime of training. Simple tricks, like foreplay and cuddling, can be magically *unlearned* at any time. Canines are loyal for life. They don't have intimacy issues. In fact, the only peace that you'll ever get from your furry friend will be when it rests in peace.

No, men are not like dogs.

They are, however, remarkably like birds!

My hands-on research has proven time and again that men are like wild things. They startle easily when you make fast moves. They'll often get very, very close to you and suddenly fly away again. When threatened, they may even become hostile or passive-aggressive and flee in an attempt to resist (emotional) arrest.

So following in the footsteps of Jane Goodall, I packed my lingerie and spent quality time in the dating wilds studying these fascinating creatures. After some painstaking (but deeply gratifying) research in the field, I've finally decoded the mating rituals of the Easily Startled Modern Male.

This book clarifies their complex mating behaviors and includes effective manhandling techniques that every woman out of a training bra *definitely* needs to know when you're looking for a husband, a boyfriend, or a plaything.

I do realize that in the past, you or a happily married girlfriend may have lucked into the perfect relationship, or a perfect dating scenario. But now that you're back in the field, you don't have to count on luck. You just need some invaluable manhandling info!

Read on and learn why:

1. The only person who can really waste your time is you!
2. It's not just who you've been dating, but how you've been dating, that's often the solution to your problem.
3. If you keep doing what you're doing, you'll just keep getting what you're getting!

(If you're thoroughly satisfied with what you've been getting, please email your findings to me! But you're probably too busy having mind-blowing sex or planning your wedding.) So for the rest of you . . .

Remember: You are now a valued member of my expert and well-dressed research team. Your romantic fulfillment is a critical factor to your well-being and happiness, so really do your homework. You'll need an open mind, a committed heart, and some lip gloss.

YOUR MISSION: As a Romantic Researcher, you'll collect data while following specific, step-by-step instructions outlining the most effective ways to conduct each fun "field experiment." You won't be out there "winging it" on your own anymore, but will learn how to approach the objects of your desire, and how to engage them, effectively.

Once you start using these tools, you'll take charge of your romantic destiny and discover that:

1. Dating isn't a mini-relationship, it's a pleasurable fact-finding mission.
2. Until he says he's The One . . . *he isn't!*

3. Dating will always result in "the survival of the fittest" when you wisely follow the laws of natural selection.

The good news is . . .

Help is on the way! If you're trapped in a romantic bog, or lost in the dark forest of singleness, fear not! In no time you'll wind up in a charming meadow, bathed in glorious sunlight and surrounded by the lovely chirping of birds.

So let's get you out of the woods so you can find your prince. 'Cause after all, every girl deserves to have a very sweaty, hot-and-heavy happy ending!

Let's go birding.

Wherever there are people there are birds, so it makes comparatively little difference where you live, if you are only in earnest about getting to know your feathered neighbors.

—Florence A. Merriam

dating

part i

"I can never tell which one of you boys is the handsomest. I was up all night trying to figure it out!"

—Anonymous

Get Flocked

Discovering the Fundamentals of Flirting

I was in that "duckling" phase. With gleaming metal braces and octagonal glasses perched upon my nose, I felt like I was destined to be awkward forever, at the tender age of eleven.

So, when my sixteen-year-old cousin arrived on our doorstep, I heard the clarion call. Linda knew the secrets of being a teenager, and wanted to know them *all*.

I studied the way that she applied blue mascara, and her trick for detangling long hair. I carried her beach bag — crammed with Teen Magazines and Coppertone — and trotted after her everywhere. (She required a Sherpa.)

Now, if her skill with makeup fascinated me, then watching her hit the beach, *mesmerized*. She was the 'preferred coordinate' for teeming flocks of handsome, suntanned boys. Wherever she went—at the volleyball nets, the Dairy Queen, or in the frigid Altantic waters— boys alighted at her side.

She was unflappable! "Thanks for the towel, Todd." she'd say with a smile, and, "Sure, Bob, I'd love a lemonade with lots and lots of chipped ice!" And she needed it, because she was on *fire*.

She didn't focus all of her attention on just one boy at a time. She was flirtatiously multi-tasking! And her worshippers didn't seem to *mind*.

"Now how did she manage that?" eleven-year-old me marvelled. I'd learn that secret, in just a few years time . . .

My cousin possessed the mindset of Flock Consciousness. By not focusing exclusively on one suitor, she attracted an entire flock of Lovebirds. She kept her options open, until she ready to choose. (Picking the right partner, takes some breathing room!)

Several years later, braces off and contacts in, I donned a halter top and a little too much blush, and went to my first high school party. I intuitively practiced what Linda had taught me and allowed a flock of boys to gather around me without making the silly mistake of getting Romantic Tunnel Vision.

This would land me a date with Paul, the star quarterback, his scent an intoxicating blend of Ivory soap and cigarettes. And also Ross, a towheaded junior who walked me home the next day after soccer practice. His dazzling white teeth would leave a small hickey that my mother would notice and ground me for later that weekend.

My romantic career had officially begun!

The One-at-a-Time Man Plan

The most common mistake that most women make is prematurely taking themselves off of the market just because "someone likes them."(Otherwise known as the One-at-a-Time Man Plan).

This misstep can happen during any phase of dating, and is a genetic holdover from the millions of years that women spent picking berries on the tundra. It'll make women want to quickly give up the hunt, and become "instantaneously monogamous" to a viable suitor once he's been found. The problem is that most men like to date women the other way *around.*

Romantic Rule: *Men, even the ones that you think are really nice guys (like architects), believe that it's not only normal, but actually preferable, to have several sexual options (women) waiting for them in the wings.*

Men don't think that this approach is wrong as long as they haven't stepped up and made a verbal commitment to any, some, or all of these women. On the contrary, most men subscribe to *The Male String Theory of Dating.*

The Male String Theory of Dating

Boys were learning much more than teamwork in Little League. They also learned the value of rotating the talent. When little boys grow up and become men, they'll apply this principle to their love lives, too. It's ingenious when you understand how it works . . .

A single male has his starting lineup of MVP's, then his Second String Girls, who like him just a little more than he likes them, and finally his Romantic Replacements, who are kept in a holding pattern on the bench.

His MVP's are usually the women he thinks he'll have mind-blowing sex with. The rest are put into romantic rotation. Men don't feel one shred of guilt about it because, after all, *they're not married*, so they don't have to act like they are. Maybe they have a point!

The Male String Theory of Dating hinges upon the *"If you're dumb enough not to ask me, I'm not gonna be stupid enough to tell you"* policy. Until men say they're clearing the deck for you with their words, they haven't made that commitment to you . . . yet. Even if their actions make them seem like they are!

Tip: It's not prying or rude to ask the men that you're dating or sleeping with about the competition you're up against, so you can to find out your real odds of contracting STDs—or actual commitments—from them! Most women are afraid of asking men what they're romantic roster is like. And you might quite be shocked by the answer, because men will often be quite happy to tell you!

MAN FACT: *Until he says he's The One, he isn't!*

What's Good for the Goose
Is Good for the Gander

I share this with you right off the bat, not because men are untrustworthy, but because it's a common dating mistake that most women get ahead of the "action."

Tip: Staying alert, holding your ground, (without shutting men down) is what creates Romantic Traction.

The Good News: If you're one of the MILLIONS of women who've been lulled into silently "wishing and waiting" or thinking you'll get what you want from men by throwing emotionally draining fits, it's helpful to look at it like this: You'd never intentionally buy the wrong size shoes. Of course you wouldn't! You'd return 'em for something that fits.

Romantic Rule: *Stop settling for the wrong sized relationship, and waiting for men to step up, that are twits!*

So without further ado, please take the *Romantic Researchers Vow.* Slip into your sexiest stilettos, put your hand on your tender heart, and say the following words aloud:

The Romantic Researcher's Hippocratic Oath

I vow to never again give the precious gift of my exclusivity to any man (no matter how rich or how hot) until he steps up and offers me the kind of relationship that I truly want. Until then, I'll be free to fly at the apex of my own flock of suitors. They'll naturally fall into a pecking order over time, until one day I notice that someone has been happily flying right beside me, who has no intention of flying south without me. And I'll have found my lovebird after all!

Now grab your handbag and follow me. Let's get flocked!

two

The Art of Flirting

Picking up whomever you want, whenever you want, can be daunting without some basic training under your garter belt. Fortunately, the art of flirting can be mastered by the prepared romantic researcher anytime, anyplace, and will transform you into the man magnet that the Goddess intends you to be!

Solo Flirting

The miracle of Online dating and dating apps have been a major boon to single women everywhere. They allow you to shop for men the same way that you'd locate Prada on eBay, with focus and intensity.

Although many couples do meet this way, women frequently complain that cyber-suitors are sometimes slightly irregular, or are so unappealing that no one else wants them, either. Quite often, the merchandise is *totally* mislabeled. A man will insist it's an XL when it's actually quite small.

Or a woman can waste several weeks flirting with an old Coot passing himself off as a jaunty Blue jay, until she finally meets the fiendish fibber in person.

That's why any woman who's serious about finding love needs to learn how to proactively flirt with all of the men in her *physical* space, as well as in cyberspace. Once you learn how to feed the birds flirtatiously, you'll never again pass up all of the dashing men who are right under your nose and dying to say hello, at the car wash . . . your vet's . . . and the local Laundromat. Flirting beats flipping through *Cat Fancy* magazine, I can promise you that!

Are You a Fantastic Flirt?

No matter how much time you spend outdoors, it will come to no avail if you're still using come-hither techniques that were in vogue sometime around the invention of the maxi pad. The following quiz will reveal if you've been relying on antiquated flirt maneuvers favored by medieval maidens-in-waiting.

Flirt Technique Diagnostic
Are the following statements True or False?

	TRUE	FALSE
If a woman makes the first move, she'll never know if a man really likes her or not.	_____	_____
If a woman initiates a first date, a man will automatically think she's looking for sex and won't respect her.	_____	_____
Men don't like to be asked out by women. They find it emasculating and a turnoff!	_____	_____

Pencils down, please.

If you answered "True" to all of the above questions, you're probably so demoralized by your lack of action that you've stopped bikini waxing!

If eating frozen yogurt is your idea of fun on a Saturday night, your salvation has finally come, hon.

MAN FACT: *There is no man shortage. Your dating technique needs an upgrade.*

Are You Flirting Like You're in a Coma?

Although modern women may not be consciously aware of it, most of us have never quite forgotten, or recovered from, the romantic coaching that we received (and often still believe) from the Brothers Grimm.

These tall tales are the cause of much of the dysfunctional, dating-disordered madness affecting most women today: the belief that finding true love should be just like a fairytale—some magical event that requires absolutely no effort on your part whatsoever. Instead, it should feel like it's been preordained by some romantic superpower, and it'll happen if it's *s'posed* to, regardless of anything you do. In fact, doing anything about it would seem kind of desperate, and just a little, well, *tacky.*

Now, let's review this for a moment together, shall we?

Once upon a time you were hanging at home in your sweats when suddenly, there was a knock on the door and . . .

Okay, I forgive any woman for getting completely sucked in by the fairytale. What woman could possibly refuse a hot prince in leotards bearing a gift of *marvelous* shoes? I can barely resist having sex with the Italian shoe salesmen in the stockroom at Bergdorf's when I'm *paying* for them.

Unfortunately, acting like a *Sleeping Beauty in a Coma* (waiting for a prince to rush in and rescue you from a life of intense boredom) is a very bad man plan. There is no data to support the idea that taking long naps and spinning flax will improve your social life whatsoever.

This way of dating—by divine intervention—seems like a good idea until I remember that unlike Sleeping Beauty, my fairy godmothers aren't casting love spells to ensure that my romantic fate will survive PMS and other acts of God.

They are at a gay bar.

And there's another big reason these tall tales are so very Grimm.

Romantic Rule: *When you flirt like a medieval maiden, you'll just wind up spinning your wheels, and the only prick you'll feel will be easily averted by a thimble!*

The Moral of the Story: In truth, the only things that most of us were paying attention to were the happy ending and the fabulous empire-waist gowns: *We just forgot to read the fine print.*

What we should have really learned from these tall tales is that there is a happy ending waiting for any woman willing to endure a little pain, alone time, self-doubt, strange companions, bizarre circumstances, and unforeseen setbacks on the way to her wedding. And some proactive flirting won't hurt you any, either.

Toss 'Em a Crumb

Most single women complain that they don't date enough, but when I ask them how many men they've asked out lately, the answer is often a shocked and confused "None!"

(Nun, get it?)

Romantic Rule: *If you want to go on more dates, "Ask and ye shall receive!" sayeth the bored.*

You can trade in your chastity belt for a garter belt and date as much as you want to, whenever you want to, when you flirt like a self-assured Romantic Researcher, and not like a Lady in Waiting.

Now, before I share maneuvers guaranteed to get you working your lingerie drawer, you'll need to trash some old ideas first. Here are two man-catching techniques as current as the crossbow and sure to keep your love life in a *very* deep sleep.

1. R.E.M.ing for Romance. Many date-free women are still trying to lure men by using Retinal Morse Code, a series of rapid eye movements, stares, and eyelash battings that signal you're there for the taking but wouldn't dream of doing the asking. This kind of passive flirting is unattractive and makes you look like you have a nervous tic. It's obviously a relic from an earlier time when women didn't have access to mascara.

2. Being a Size Queen. Millions of women spend gorgeous weekends at SoulCycle hoping that their dream man will magically appear the very second they can fit back into their skinny jeans. These women blame the size of their thighs for their singleness, and believe that when they finally look perfect, the Barbie Dream House will become theirs, along with Ken and all of those fabulous shoes! I'll let you in on a little secret. Even women who are 4's are often date-free too! That's why every woman, no matter how small or how tall, will benefit from acquiring modern flirt technology.

MAN FACT: *No man can tell just by looking at you that you're available and single. He'll cut his odds of rejection way down by waiting for you to send him a tiny smoke signal of approval, before he makes his move!*

That's why every single woman needs to master the fun Art of Flirting!

WARNING: In the following chapter, you'll learn how to get positively *flocked* with male attention, so don't say I didn't warn you!

Feed the Birds

You can date as much as you want to, whenever you want to, by mastering the art of the magical phrase "Nice tie!" This maneuver can be performed by the solo flirter anytime, anyplace, and is guaranteed to transform you into the man magnet that the Goddess intended you to be!

How to Become a Magical Man Magnet

The next time that an intriguing man crosses your path, simply compliment something he's *wearing* or *doing*. All men love to be admired. They are totally motivated by it, will go to war for it, and build skyscrapers for it, so all you have to do is use this male character trait to your romantic advantage.

Casting a small crumb of approval a man's way will have an amazing 'open sesame' effect on him. He will happily chirp away with any woman smart enough to notice his fine feathers . . . and waterproof sports watch.

MAN FACT: *Men are externally referenced. They cuddle up with magazines about breasts, cars, and guns. Conversing with men about any gizmo, gadget, or inanimate object is always the best way to draw them out.*

WARNING : Never compliment a man on his physique! This will only serve to embarrass or confuse him about what your intentions are. (Unless he's way too young for you. Then we know what your plans are for him are, so go right ahead and spell it out for him!)

The secret to breaking the ice is to make sure that your compliment is always once removed. (Exceptions: tattoos and huge biceps. They fall under the purview of man jewelry, too.)

TRUE STORY: I once said, "Nice tie," to a gorgeous man on the red carpet at a film premiere. He whipped it off and proudly handed it to me, to the amazement of his little entourage. *(I used it to tie him to my bedpost one rainy evening . . . but I'll tell you that story later.)*

Luring Your Lovebird

After you've engaged a man in light conversation about his car, sneakers, or tie, he may spontaneously ask for your phone number. But what if he's flapping around a bit and isn't confident about coming in for a landing?

WARNING: Only proceed if your first compliment was snapped right up. If it was, throw him this crumb . . .

"We should get a cup of tea sometime!"

Now before you get your knickers in a twist, consider this. Meeting for tea is a very low-risk, because your intentions are vague.

You aren't asking him to meet you at a strip club. You aren't even asking him to meet you for a drink! You're inviting him to have a proper cup of tea, like Jane Austin absolutely would. He'll quickly jump to the conclusion that you are (a) a lady and (b) fascinating!

I guarantee that no woman has ever asked him out for a cup of tea before. Unless he's a Brit. (They love *"teatime"* too!) It will make him feel a little confused (this is good) and all sparkly inside.

Or you could just breezily say, *"Let's get together and discuss global warming!"* This will make him laugh, (this is good!) and you'll not only have a potentially great date, but also help to save the *planet.*

Romantic Rule: Don't ever ask a man out for a drink, lunch, or dinner. It's presumptuous and will only put you at a dating disadvantage later. Always leave it to men to upgrade a teatime request.

If your Lovebird's been following the trail of breadcrumbs you've been tossing his way, he'll cheerily hop a little closer and chirp, *"That'd be great!"* This is your cue to say, in the most offhanded way, *"Do you have a card, Bernard?"*

I know this might sound a bit old-fashioned, but that's a part of its charm. And luckily, there are only four possible responses to this question:

1. **"Yes"**. He quickly hands his card over. Brightly say, *"Great, I'll give you a call, Paul."*

WARNING: Just tuck it into your purse and smile. Never try to set up a date with a man at this time unless he instigates it. This is a rule.

2. *"I don't have a card, but here's my ___ "* (Cellphone, IG, or What's App number, etc.)

Which should always be followed by him saying...

3. *"Let me get your contact info! I'll hit you up!"*

He quickly asks for your contact info too, *et voila!* You get a Manhandling Gold Star, and he does too.

Or ...

4. *He turns tail and disengages before doing so.*

This won't ever happen, but if it does do not fret, and don't push. Just let him fly away! It's of no consequence to you.

It simply means that you look like his hot bipolar ex-girlfriend who ruined his life when she went off her meds, or that he's already been banded (married).

You won't ever know the reason why he let you slip through his fingers, and quite frankly, we don't want to know. Just say, while quickly gliding away: *"It was a delight to meet you, André. Have a fabulous day!"*

MANHANDLING MANEUVER: If your subject 'fesses up and says he's currently involved with someone, never be embarrassed that you flattered him with your attention. Things couldn't have gotten to this stage unless he was flirting right back at you! It's actually *his* fault that you're both in this predicament, and he's offering an explanation as a way of eating crow. Just say, *"Lucky girl!"* and smile, while looking him dead in the eye. Consider it a moment of triumph, and then immediately exit stage left.

WARNING: If a banded or already "tagged" male tries to set up a date with you at this juncture, do not accept! You will incur *incredibly bad dating karma* if you do. If you entertain these kinds of invitations, or worse, encourage them, call me immediately. You need a little psychic tune-up. I'll probably be out in the field, but I do have a very soothing outgoing message.

Any Questions?

Q: Why should I ask a man out? I want a guy who has enough balls to ask me out!

A: Well, I wish the ice caps weren't melting, but they are. In a perfect world things would be, well, perfect. But in the real world men are distracted, rumpled, in terrible need of a shave. And sometimes a nudge. According to *Cosmo* magazine, 78 percent of men polled said they loved it when women made the first moves, and didn't think any less of the women who made them. So there you have it. I rest my case.

Okay? Any more questions?

Q: But won't he think I'm a slut if I ask him out for tea?

A: He'll think you're a slut if you *act* like a slut. No one is asking you to behave like one, so don't! (Unless you want to. Then enjoy!)

Fun Fact: Manolo Blahnik once said, "I love sluts. They are the kindest people in the world." And obviously very well-heeled, too.

Oh, all right, one more question. You there...in the back?

Q: *Maybe the Universe doesn't want me to be with anyone. If it does, I'm sure it'll send someone along. And if not, it's probably just not meant to be ... right?*

A: Wow, the Universe, although extremely busy, just sent me this note to pass along to you.

Dear Needing a Sign,

We, the Universal Powers That Be, want you to be wildly happy and sexually fulfilled. But we're extremely busy managing black holes and DNA strands and trying to ensure that most of you keep driving on the right side of the road. So we'd really appreciate it if you took the lead in your personal fulfillment; but we do promise to send little clues when you're on the right track—and small, unexpected shoves in the right direction and we, the Universe, promise to cry at your wedding.

Signed,

The Universal Powers That Be
(very interested in you!)

three

Get Your Ducks
In a Row

If a man has taken your phone number or IG handle but he's also gallantly slipped you his, just go get a manicure and let him contact you *first*. When you both swap cell numbers or private contact info in any of its forms (with the exception of dating apps where the same rules do not apply), classic *Stone Age Dating Etiquette* still reigns supreme.

Stone Age Dating Etiquette: Man Hunts. Woman Gathers.

(Don't try to reinvent the wheel!)

MAN FACT: *Both men and dogs love chasing balls and shiny objects. When something captures their attention, they'll chase it! (Unless they're married, and trying to stay that way.)*

So to keep things simple: Put. Down. Your. Cellphone.

If you have itchy trigger finger, take up knitting.Everyone loves receiving a holiday scarf!

After every outing, deposit all of your collections (business cards) into a sterile container (card file). You can wave a little wand over it several times and say, "May there be a Lovebird among these toads."

Then let him incubate for four days before sending him a proactive text to his mobile number, or a short and sweet email (see below), or a Linked-In message as a last resort!

Why wait four days to make contact, you might ask? Why not two days, or even three? If you're wondering if this rule is a whim, let me assure you that all of my manhandling intel is based on the most up-to-date romantic research.

Check out these results from the latest GQ poll . . .

How Long Should a Guy Wait to
Call a Girl After Getting Her
                          Number?
Instantly 50%

One day: 40%

Two days: 10%

MAN FACT: *When men meet you, whether they just want to shag you, date you, (or both), they'll connect with you ASAP. They know that quickly following up, makes women feel great!*

This call back time- frame isn't as effective for women, when they'd like to approach *men,* however. Many women botch a perfectly good romantic prospect and opportunity because they just "wing it" with "Let's jump on it!" intensity. While you may always mirror a man's level of interest, never feel pressured to mimic the Modern Males calling, texting, or flirting patterns, by reaching out to men instantly. They're not going anywhere! You'll want to create *intrigue,* not predictability.

Now, curiosity may have killed the cat, but it's totally purr-rfect for luring a Lovebird. So take away his cocksureness and create some mystery by giving him just enough time to wonder where you are. And to kick himself for not getting your last name, or your phone number!

Congratulations! You have become elusive, a prize, and have potentially magnetized him to you. You have just created:

INTRIGUE n 1. an involved plot to achieve your ends. 2. a clandestine love affair with a hot man in a foreign country who says things to you in bed that you don't understand, but like! 3. cause him to be terribly interested in you.

But if you have his card or contact info and he doesn't have yours, here's the perfect way to cast a love spell:

Contact a new prospect on day four between 2 and 5 pm.
It's unwise to call a strange bird in the morning or late at night. Don't intrude on his personal time. Instead, shoot him a text or an email midafternoon. He'll be settled back into his work and won't be hungry. (It is always unwise to surprise a man who hasn't eaten, unless you're nude or have access to food.) **Important Tip:** You're only ringing him up to say hello! Allow men to ask you out for a date, if he so chooses. He's the dude! Okay? So let's make his day . . .

Love Script - How to Make Your Move . . .
Grab your phone and text him something like this: "Hey there, Tim. It's Lucy Fur, the girl who you rescued from boredom at the D.M.V. How are you?"

Congrats! You've passed him the ball, and he should text-message or email, call or email you right back. If there's anything to make a wry joke about, certainly do. Humor is a great social lubricant!

Now comes the moment of truth.

The Lucky Duck texts right back and is thrilled to hear from you. He may even say that he was about to stake out wherever it was that he met you in the hopes of bumping into you again. This happens to all of my Romantic Research team members constantly. Well done! You've lured yourself a Lovebird! This Lucky Duck won't let you slip through his hands twice, and will usually upgrade your date from teatime to something more romantic (and substantial), like cocktails or dinner.

But sometimes, you might've drawn in a wingnut . . .

The Blackout Drinker seems to have trouble remembering who you are. If things escalate to an actual phone call and he still can't place who you are, just say, *"I can't hear you...uh-oh... sorry, my cell is cutting out!"* and quickly hang up. This isn't rude on your *part*. After all, he flirted with you, gave you his card, and is now pretending that he *doesn't remember you*. As *if!* Don't waste one more second on him. This man doesn't need a date, he needs rehab!

The Iceman Cometh. You call and he pleasantly twitters away without asking you for your number or trying to set up a date. Because *he's married*. And now that he's sober, he's remorseful. Don't waste one more second on him, and just toss it off! Say, *"Ah! Sorry, my boyfriend is calling and I've gotta run. But it was a pleasure chatting! Goodbye, and good luck!"*

What you're much more likely to hear, however, sounds like this: *"Hi there! I was hoping that you'd call. Are you free this weekend?"* Gold star, and game on!

Birds on the Wire

Always follow these (unbreakable) rules when texting new flock members . . .

The Cloak of Silence. In the beginning stages of courtship, do not initiate contact with men first. If you've gone out on a date with them or have met them in person and they like you, they'll contact you! Do feel free to respond quickly and with enthusiasm when they reach out to you, however! Just don't see them that same evening, (unless he's got *amazing* concert tickets, or wants to take you to Vienna).

Playing "hard to get" will make it too hard to connect with you, once you're already dating. It's always okay to respond to a call or a text right away, especially if it regards an imminent plan.

If he starts blowing up your phone with texts and you've either just met, or worse, you haven't had a real date yet, delay responding or several hours, or the next day. Hey, you have a life! Or you're going to start acting "as if" and pretend that you do!

Starting-And-Stopping Mid-Text? No explanation needed! Pretend it was a "cyber-whoops" if he dare to ask!

69ing. As for *69, ignore this calling feature entirely. I don't like to encourage it in the bedroom, either. It's like allowing your man to drive drunk. He needs to be alert to stay in the lane! You should be *way too busy* to worry about random phone numbers popping up on your phone. But if someone keeps calling and hanging up, just call 'em back and say, "*Dr. Klein, is that you? Are my pregnancy test results back?*"

VM Interception. This is a real lifesaver. If you see his number and your heart turns over because his call comes as a shock, or you're way too crushed-out to talk in complete sentences, call him back when you stop hyperventilating. It's the modern version of fainting.

Chickening Out When Calling Him. Aka the "OHMYGOD" reflex. Just call when you're ready, and say you got cut off by an incoming call!

four

Assembling Your Mantrap Pack

It's now time to organize what we at the Institute of Romantic Research refer to as a **Mantrap Pack.** Besides being effective, going on a Manhunt with dedicated wing women can be even more fun than shoe shopping!

YOUR MISSION: Having and epic GNO (Girls Night Out) while your spotting and luring Lovebirds. Now that you have my flirting technology at your fingertips, you can get flocked absolutely anywhere, anytime, together!

Note: Always remember that you're on a mission. Your happiness and future fulfillment may hang in the balance. Countless relationships and marriages have resulted from exactly this kind of focused and synchronized group fieldwork. Stay alert, flirters!

Casting Your Mantrap Pack

Size matters. (But you already knew that!) The ideal number for a Mantrap Pack is four because it's just perfect for splitting up and double-teaming. Never go flirting with five or more women, however. That amount of estrogen is way too potent and will turn your mantap pack expedition into a vivacious girls' night out.

Good casting is essential. Begin by asking your most man motivated girlfriends if they would like to become part of your "expert and well-dressed research team." Clue: This should be met with an enthusiastic "Hell, yes!"

Top-drawer candidates for a Mantrap Pack. They're supportive and available for consistent and ongoing fieldwork. Needless to say, you'll only want to invite a true-blue Girls' Girl into a 'birding group.'*

A Note to New Team Leaders: Not every woman is ideally suited for this task. Try as you will, experience is always the best teacher. You'll find your casting has gone awry if you observe the following:

The Man Hater. She creates a psychic No-Fly Zone that blocks handsome men from approaching and entering your airspace because of her terrifically bad vibe. Men can spot a Man Hater on their radar from miles away and will instinctively back off. She is like romantic kryptonite and can stop any man mid-flight, causing him to plummet to the earth like a stone.

---

* The Girls' Girl knows that although love affairs may be brief, girlfriends are forever. The Girls' Girl would never dream of letting some hot piece of ass ruin your friendship. She would never ever bed your boyfriend, even if he was really hot and they were both drunk and left all alone on a beach in Tahiti. Girls' Girls are not full of envy or jealousy, but enjoy tea parties at Starbucks, and have learned how to share their toys. This lady's got your back.

How to diagnose a Man Hater: You lure men in, but she either acts distant and standoffish, tries to pick a fight with them—or begins to argue with you instead! Men will break through this force field of hate if they find you amazingly attractive, but why set up an obstacle course for them to navigate? If you find this saboteur in your midst, demote her lovingly back to girlfriend status and leave her at home with the remote while you're out on the prowl.

You'll also find that your casting went awry if you discover:

The Man Eater: She views romance as a competition and won't mind sleeping with your boyfriend whether she's drunk *or* sober. After all, if he was really into you, he wouldn't be cheating on you, right? The Man Eater is a terrible candidate for a Mantrap Pack. She only pledges allegiance to her own flag. Never engage in three ways with this woman! She'll be delighted to steal your boyfriend.

Private consultation for the Man Eater: If you're a Man Eater, you obviously don't need a Man- trap Pack. You're already packing and can use these manhandling tips all by yourself. Just try to wield your power wisely. If you're reading this book, I can only assume that the prospect of world domination has lost some of its glow, and you're ready for a happy ending that lasts longer than three minutes. Hey, you deserve to be happy. Just don't steal everyone else's toys.

And finally, be sure to sidestep . . .

The Dater Player Hater. This little wet blanket thinks that any dating effort is totally futile. Although lovely in every other respect, the Dater Player Hater is a black hole of negativity when it comes to the topic of men. She has a mental loop that automatically derails any effort you make to cheer her up about her love life. She would rather be *right* than happy. "I would *never date anyone that* I met in a bar," she'll mutter while you're sipping your martini and flirting with two cute men. *At a bar!* This woman is way too much work. Don't let her torpedo your romantic plans. Just give her Das Boot.

   Any Questions?

Q: *Do all the members of a Mantrap Pack have to be single?*

   A: **Absolutely not! You can always bring a Decoy.** Your team members don't have to be looking for love themselves to be amazingly effective. In fact, married woman will often volunteer to perform some of the most dangerous flirtatious field ops. She'll go way out on a limb for you because she has nothing to lose. (Well, maybe her pride, but she won't really mind because she's already taken, and married women just love to fix up single girls; it almost borders on a sickness!). They're like little suicide bombers of love, with nothing at stake except your happiness. They're fabulous teammates!

   According to statistics, meeting men with your gal pals while you're out and about, is one of the top three ways that formerly single women met the men they married, dated, or snogged. So get busy!

   And now that you've assembled your Romantic Research Team, let's get you on the front lines. And you might want to slip on your stiletto's . . .

five

Flirting in the field

The following flirt maneuvers can be used by your Mantrap Pack, and will also work perfectly when you're flirting solo, too! They're guaranteed to increase your confidence, fill out your fine flock, and are oh-so-much-fun to do!

Romantic Rule: *Men, like birds, are everywhere! Look about!*

Get a bird's-eye view of the room.

I cannot stress the importance of using this time-saving technique enough! Climb directly to the highest vantage point possible in any venue, (positioning yourself at the top of the stairs at a club, or leaning on the railing of a balcony to quickly survey the terrain and assess the talent.)

You can even use a pair of small opera glasses, like women in Versailles used to do! If you're at a concert, walk right up to the stage and then turn around, *et voilà!* The entire room will now be facing *you*. A good lookout can quickly turn any vantage point to her "romantic advantage."

Never sit with your back to a room. You won't meet them if you can't greet them, so always position your Pack to easily spot *Incomings*, (aka handsome men).

Never place yourself in a secluded or quiet area of a bar or restaurant. Instead, position yourself in high-traffic areas by requesting a table or barstool close to the front-line action.

Keep exploring. If you're at a club or an event and it's a dud, skip out and move on to the next. Hey, that's why they call it going on a Manhunt! Always coordinate your team's itinerary and plan at least three man-friendly destinations to explore per mission, if you find the men at your present locale are too "low-tide at the gene pool."

Peer about. You can always pretend to be looking for someone. *(You are! You just haven't met him yet.)* Begin at one corner of a room and then do a complete lap around the perimeter. If you're in a crowded venue, do this every twenty minutes!

Scout them out. One of you should volunteer to play the role of Scout. Scouts keep tabs on exotic birds on the move and perform "covert ops" that provide valuable intel for what would otherwise devolve into romantic misfires. Scouts do a quick lap around the room, and then immediately return and give great field reports, like: "Forget it, babe. He just bought a drink for that girl at the bar." Or, "Your in luck! She just left with another dude. Let's shimmy on over, and see what you think!"

Don't forget high-volume areas. Lobbies and concession stands are excellent places to Mantrap, and are commonly overlooked by the inexperienced flirter. If you're at a convention or conference, they're a fabulous place to strike up a chat!

Falconing

You can attract birds to your nest with just a little work by using the **Come-Hither Hand Signal** ®, my patented man-magnet system. This gesture is guaranteed to penetrate across any crowded room and right into the heart of even the most intimidating man cluster.

MANHANDLING MANEUVER: The Come-Hither Hand Signal®

The Lure: Command him invitingly. Get a handsome man in your sights. Look him straight in the eye, while crooking your finger in a come-hither motion and give him a tiny smile. Men find this gesture irresistible because it's utterly sexy and confident; they will fly to you like Falcons!

The Bait: When he lands at your side, smile and say, *"Nice tie! This is my girlfriend Courtney."*

The Hand Off: Turn to your grateful girlfriend and say, *"I'm going to go find Stacy. I'll be back in a minute."*

Then Take Off: Buzz off! They'll either exchange pleasantries and drift apart, or exchange phone numbers. And either way, good for you! You are an awesome girlfriend.

You can always use the Come-Hither Hand Signal to lure men directly to *your* side, too. Although this might sound daunting, it's actually quite fun and so easy to do, (and excellent training for the inner dominatrix in you!)

ManTrap Pack Maneuvers
(Romantic Reports from the Field)

The following **Playerette Positions** are tactical maneuvers that can only be accomplished by a smooth-running unit. After just a little practice, the results will be stunning. And remember to send me your field reports!

Mantrap Pack Migration

Sometimes you'll notice that some Lame Duck starts to orbit your Mantrap Pack, and tries to cockblock the handsome males you'd rather give clearance to. This situation was quickly remedied by a savvy Los Angeles–based Mantrap Pack.

Shooting Down Wild Turkeys

"We noticed an undesirable tracking us all night, but we just couldn't shake him off our tail. He kept eavesdropping and performing unwanted surveillance. We followed standard protocol and did a **Mantrap Pack Migration** (positional relocation to the other side of the bar), but this Turkey just waddled after us in hot pursuit. So I pulled the trigger and shot the sucker down.

I looked that Wild Turkey straight in the eye, and said, 'Hey, we're having a private conversation, but have a good night!" And then we all swiftly turned our backs on him in unison.

Unfortunately, he was a cling-on. So I said, with energy, 'Dude, my friend just got of prison for arson, and we're celebrating. *Au revoir!*" That got our team dweeb-free immediately!"

The Human Shield
Field Report from Las Vegas

"Our pack was at a concert one night when our Scout, Marilee spotted a very hot Swede smiling at her. She also spied another girl desperately trying to get his attention. She quickly gave the verbal signal, "Mascara!" and we swiftly repositioned ourselves to block the visual sight path between her target and the interloper.

Operation: Target His Wingmen. Then our Mantrap Pack quickly circled the wagons by using the magical phrase "*Nice sportswear!*" to distract his wingmen.

The "Divide and Conquer." Soon the rest of us were chatting up his friends. They were gorgeous, too! (Sometimes being selfless really is its own reward!) This left the sexy Swede free, and Marilee stepped right in, much to his delight.

So what happened next?

They hit it off and wound up dating for three steamy weeks before Sven had to go surfing in Bali. But before he left, he certainly waxed her board!"

Excellent work, ladies, and thanks for the report!

Romantic Rule: Never allow Lame Ducks to cockblock handsome men from entering your airspace. Always shoot down the pests, and keep your landing strip free and clear.

(This goes for bikini waxing, too, my dear.)

six

Sitting Ducks

Let's go on a manhunt!

If you want to find a Bird of Paradise, you probably won't spot him at your local Taco Bell. Serious birdwatchers know that targeted Manhunting expeditions increase the odds of landing the Lovebirds they most desire.

Romantic Rule: When it comes to Manhunting, "winging it" is for the birds.

Targeted treks are often best done on weekend afternoons in man-rich locations. Adventuresome and dedicated flirters will soon discover that "getting out of your bubble" will yield fabulous results. The key is to travel off the beaten paths used by every other woman in your neighborhood. If you're game enough to leave your comfort zone, however, you'll discover some amazing opportunities to meet handsome men, and it'll be will be way more fun than organizing your sock drawer.

Upside for Afternoon Birding: Any man who falls for you when you're wearing jeans and a ponytail will be just wild about you when you're 'evening fabulous.*'

Romantic Rule: Change your routine and go where the men are. Improving your male-to-female ratio will always up your odds of romantic success!

Planning Your Expedition

Round up your Mantrap Pack and then plan your campaign over cocktails by asking each member to specify the type of fellow that she'd most love to find!. Organize your outings to accommodate all of you, or pair off specialized jaunts once you declare your "type" and preferences, like trekking to the Opera to find Condors and Penguins, for example.

Here are some helpful (and actual!) birding terms:

TARGET BIRDS: Are at the top of your list and the men that you most desire.

ACCIDENTALS: Are the fellows you'd never expect to find in this strange locale, like running your shopping-cart into Bradley Cooper's backside at your local grocery store.

NEMESIS BIRDS: These are exasperating Target Birds that keep eluding your grasp even though you've been in hot pursuit of them. (Examples: The Nesting Lovebird, the Homing Pigeon, or the Master Cock).

---

*"I was just in my workout clothes!" "I was wearing my sloppy sweater." "I didn't have a stitch of makeup on!" This is taken from studies we conducted on first meetings that led to marriages: 97 percent of the successful birders surveyed remarked!

Bird Sanctuaries:

18 Top Notch Places To Spot Lovebirds

1. Cyberspace! Dating apps and sites are a virtual man catalogue in the sky. You'll have (literally) millions of men at your manicured fingertips. Dating apps like Hinge, Tinder and Bumble are the new Match.coms of the past, and not (just) for hookups. When you know how to market yourself and flirt effectively here, it's almost as fun as finding a pair of vintage boots on eBay, and ultimately, even more rewarding!

MANHANDLING MANEUVER: Stop getting carpal tunnel on Tinder! Check out my "Secrets to Dating In Cyberspace!" and my Man Magnet Makeovers at www.laurenfrances.com. They'll up your odds of finding the One, hon!

Create the right bait to attract the right mate!
Profile photo's are like romantic Rorschach tests. A picture says a thousand words, and if your photos don't pop, it won't really matter what you write. (Sorry!) If you don't look happy in your photo's, men will assume that you're either angry, depressed, remote, or sad, so remember to smile!

Tip: Go to www.CupidsInbox.com and get my complimentary podcasts and tip-sheets and you'll soon get flocked with fabulous online suitors. They're right in my Love Store!
(Over 1M downloads, baby!)

2. Sporting Events. Men enjoy playing with balls, and love watching other men play with them too. Stadium games are virtual bird-a-thons, teeming with huge flocks or breeding males who migrate here year-round.

Caveat: You must be willing to embrace a relationship that revolves around banners, beer, and barbecue. But you'll know where to find him!

The Upside: "Sport birding" automatically gives you that Gisele Bundchen Factor, even if you're not 5'11"and leggy, and married to Tom Brady.

Birdwatching: If you like pro athletes, get a spray-tan and crash VIP parties celebrating the rare Condors and athletic Master Cocks who have temporarily touched down in your area, if you're game!

3. The Local Basketball Court.

It's so fun to watch men playing pickup games *(I mean, really!)* on the weekends. Smart birders come to view the local males strutting their stuff on their neighborhood courts.

Bonus: You'll get to check out their six-packs without having to get naked, too!

BODY BAIT: Borrow a friend's dog and play fetch near the nets. Canines are an all purpose icebreaker!

4. The Apple Store. This place is always teeming with men, looking for gadgets and gizmos. Ask a cute Lovebird for help. He may be as confused as you are, but he'll pretend *not* to be. (Cute!) All species of birds convene here, from Horned Owls to Robins. This borders on man-catching genius. (The same rules apply for Restoration Hardware.)

5. Watering Holes. Peacocks, Robins, and Bushtits all group together in loose flocks and spend their evenings foraging for women in these intoxicating wetlands. Listen for their drunken chirrup as they move from one watering hole to another in pursuit of nighttime fun.

6. Grocery Stores, Juice Bars, Coffee Shops. Go directly to "guy-friendly" food sections which include, but are not limited to: frozen foods, canned soups, soda and beer aisles, bagged chips and treats, and the deli section for Boomers, and fresh veggies and juice bars to spot cute millennials!

7. Hardware Stores. These are easy places to strike up a conversation with any man. If one of your Mantrap Pack members likes a fellow who's handy with his tools, go right between the hammers and the nails.

The Upside: Men that you meet in hardware stores *already do chores.* And they're often homeowners. (A win-win!)

True Story: I was once looking through paint swatches for my bedroom at Home Depot when a ridiculously hot man peered over my shoulder and asked me what color I was leaning toward. "Pink," I replied. "It's the international color of welcome." He laughed and the rest is history. (Read more in *The Confessions of Dr. Elle.*)

MANHANDLING MANEUVERS: Think of something in your home that needs improving, then ask a handsome man to help you find and operate a ratchet, a wrench, duct tape, oh, anything really. Accept his kind offer to help, if you like him!

Man Tackle: Always wear high heels to Home Depot. This is a rule!

8. The gym and beyond: A variety of species converge at the local gym to create a spectacular dawn chorus. Go birding early in the morning and see who's motivated enough to buff up before work. And you can check out the merch!

The Upside: Most early birds have jobs. And if you go to the pool, you can check out his trunk(s) as it'll be easy to spot.

Tip: Man-heavy workout destinations like boxing gyms and martial arts classes can be fabulous fun. Ask the manager if you can observe the class before joining, and check out the talent.

WARNING: Many metro-sexual males are now flocking to Soul Cycle, yoga and Pilates classes too. At least they're flexible . . . and smart. Notice how Yoga Boy is throwing the odds in his favor by invading the hen house. *(Beward of falling for a Pink Flamingo.)*

9. Sports Bars, Cigar Bars & Pool Halls.
Dodo's and Woodpeckers will compete for your attention at the pool table's edge. Full of raucous chirping and crowing, the sports bar is a perfect destination for a fun Mantrap expedition. Robin Redbreasts, Larks, Loons, and Homing Pigeons will be in full view, too. It's a free for all!

Tip: Find out the dates and times of big stakes games and make a reservation well in advance if they take 'em!

Body Bait: Only slow dancing with a stranger is sexier than having him watch you work a big (cue) stick.

10. Men's Department Stores. Men are often dazed and confused in this locale and are often found waddling around. Peer through the dense (clothing) cover to spot him. Stay alert! He may be a rare find. At least he likes to go shopping!

MANHANDLING MANEUVER: *Ask him for help. Say:"You look like you're the same size as my brother. Would you mind trying this on?" or "Do you like this cologne? I can't tell if it's man-friendly."*

11. Driving Ranges, Tennis Courts, and Squash Courts. This is the perfect place to meet active(ish) well-heeled men.

MANHANDLING MANEUVER: *Ask some lucky fella to help you improve your stroke or swing.*

Body Bait: Wear something ass-tastic!

12. Fundraisers. These events provide reliable opportunities to bump into some rarefied, desirable and otherwise hard-to-locate men. But they are also often banded! (Married). It is an excellent way to network, and you can always volunteer or join their board. (And you get brownie points from me for being a great person!)

The Upside: You never know who has an amazing son or nephew that needs a fix up! Just say "Yes! I'd be delighted to meet him. What can I bring to dinner?"

Body Bait: Make sure a Pink Flamingo helps you accessorize. Getting all dolled up for mantrapping's tons of fun!

13. Google & Facebook, IG Meetups:

Local singles events are easy to search for online, and try doing a search for *Meet Up Groups* for man-friendly activities. River rafting, mountain biking, rock climbing, surfing, and the like. This is a great and low-pressure way to meet men, and get your butt in great shape!

14. The Beach.

Shorebirds of all types flock here in droves. The summer months are the easiest way to spot love-birds of all breeding species, everywhere.

WARNING: It's easier to identify males ages (Juvenille or Nesting) without their plumage (clothing) which can be confusing when they're fully dressed (and be incorrectly classified, altogether).

MANHANDLING MANEUVER: *Undo your bikini top and say, "Can you pass me the sunblock? Ohhh, I can't reach my back . . . thanks for your help!"*

15. Nightclubs.

Bring your binoculars while birding in this classic male sanctuary. Almost anything is liable to turn up here, from lovely Homing Pigeons and Robins at the bar, Sparrows trying to just get in the door, to the American Bushtit (I did not make this bird up. Google it), along with a stunning variety of Master Cocks in the V.I.P. section.

Man Tackle: Wear stilettos!

16. ComicCon.

This convention is just swarming with men, nerds, fanboys, and celebrities. He might be wearing a costume when you meet him, but who am I to judge?

Man Tackle: Dress like Wonder Woman and men will flock to you in droves.

17. Events, Expos, Lectures, Classes and Tournaments.
Research outings with your wing-women, and you'll have a ball, flirting together.

Bowling and fly-fishing tournaments, the local rodeo, heavy metal reunions, big-rig racing, demolition derbies, extreme sports competitions, science lectures, money market and investment seminars, automotive expos. Local papers and magazines (like *Time's Out*) list art gallery openings, concerts, theatre, gala's and other ecclectic local events, like pie eating competitions.

You get the idea. Go to events that you would *never* have thought of attending. Who knows? You might just wind up with a passion for restoring vintage cars, and snag yourself a hot hubby, too.

When you go on targeted dating treks with your Mantrap Pack, you'll soon have a lively flock of suitors teeming all about you. Flirt your butt(s) off and have tons of fun hunting men in their natural habitats, Pussycat!

seven

Male Courtship Displays

The first several dates should be light, fun, and romantic. Your man should confirm your date well in advance, make reservations, and restrain himself from trying to bone you like a fish. Any deviation from this time-tested formula is always a red flag. A man earns a woman's affection through proper care and consistent attention. On a first date, and every date, a man should impress you with his ability to care *for you* and *about* you.

MAN FACT: Men invest in the things that they value with the resources they have at their disposal, be it cash, creativity, energy, or enthusiasm.

Always notice if he's rowing through the air first with one wing and then the other, to win your affection, or cruising right along with sails set. If he makes plans that are insultingly casual, doesn't compliment you, (or worse, is unaffectionate), it's a clear sign that he's withholding his approval and lowering your expectations. He won't be properly courting you!

Take his lackluster performance seriously, and shoo him right out of your nest without further ado. You certainly won't miss him.

(*See* Arctic Tern, Mockingbird, and Peckish Mute Warblers.)

MAN FACT: The plans that a man *makes* for you, tell you the plans that he *has* for you!

Mating Calls and Warning Signels

A Long lead time. The considerate male always calls or texts you well in advance. He knows that you're too in demand to have huge holes in your calendar, and he'll want to make sure to reserve some of this valuable time for himself.

A Confirming Call. You should always receive a confirming text or phone call before 3 p.m. on Date Day. Enthused and thoughtful men text women the day before, and often when they're en route. If there will be any delay, you should be notified well in advance. If he calls after 6 p.m. on D-Day, tell him you would love to see him, but that you've just made other plans. But you'd be delighted to see him next Thursday!

A Little Planning. It's always a good sign when a man has made reservations for a first date. It's proof that he isn't winging it and can organize himself enough to think about you, make a plan, and then stick to it. Beware the girly-man who asks in a whiny voice what *you'd* like to do. He's either lacking in testosterone or motivation, or he just wants to have sex with you and then quickly move on.

The exceptions to this are when you've both connected via a dating app or online. Then the bar for first dates can be literally, pretty low! Just don't agree to meet for coffee someplace sloppy. Suggest a lovely resto, hotel bar, or a gorgeous lobby. If you haven't met him yet in person, relax. You're not on your second date . . . yet.

MAN FACT: Men who don't make fun reservations for you often have reservations *about* you. And sometimes, you'll start having reservations about them!

And if you're wondering who should pick up the check, consider this, Miss .

REALITY CHECK: Women spend wads of money on first dates: there's bikini waxing (painful), manicure and blow-drys (time-consuming), lingerie (expensive), and Pilates (ridiculously over-priced). It's a serious investment for women to show up for date one. The very least a man can do is pick up the check and feed you!

A Lovebird should arrive at your date destination before you do (aka on time). Never allow strangers men you haven't met in person yet to pick you up, or know your home address, or workplace. That info is reserved for men that you feel totally comfortable with. But if he has passed the first date test, the man's not a Loon.

Romantic Rule: It's always bad form for a man to keep you waiting, in general, but especially so on a first or a second (or any) date.

This always throws me into complete Dressing Disorder. This occurs when your date is so late that you keep changing your clothes until the doorbell rings, and are then forced to greet him mid-outfit! We blame this on the tardy man, who really should've arrived on time, to avert this fashion crisis.

TRUE STORY: I once had man ring my bell twenty-two minutes late, who looked me over and had the nerve to say, "Wow, you look like you're ready to perform in an off-Broadway show!"

The Upside: I was disinclined to allow him into my bedroom, which was now utterly strewn with dresses and shoes.

Now really, if a man can manage to arrive at work on time and plant his ass in front of the TV in time for the playoffs, he can ring your doorbell on time, right? After all, you're big game, too!

Here's a good rule of thumb: Although men should absolutely be on time, women are always allowed to be a little late. That's why men are already at waiting for us at the altar, and not the other way around! All men know that you have Dressing Disorder, too. Now, don't you feel better?

I certainly do.

eight

Strutting

In the bird kingdom, the male struts his stuff and displays his fine feathers to get the female's attention. The male mating dance is a highly evolved ritual.

BIRD FACT: Have you ever wondered why the peacock's tail has so many eyes? It's because he wants to get laid! His girlfriends, aka peahens, are fascinated by the large staring eyes on the tails of their gorgeous suitors. They actually put her into a mild state of hypnosis, making it much easier for the peacock to lunge at her.

Therefore, the more eyes he has on his tail, the more irresistible the peahen will find him. It is only logical that peacocks have evolved larger and larger eyes on their tails to exploit her preference. And to get some peahen love.

The same is true for men. They'll try to seduce you at exotic restaurants, ply you with alcohol, and make up transparent excuses to get you to nip into their mansions after dinner. Male posturing is a mating directive emanating from deep within his reptilian brain, even if he's wearing Armani.

So, all of you women in the wild should certainly bare this in mind . . .

MAN FACT: *A man who isn't trying to impress you isn't very impressed with you.*

Strutting Their Stuff and the Male Need for Approval

When a man goes into "breeding mode," he'll automatically start to strut his stuff. He does this by telling you how he destroyed the competition at the board meeting, vanquished a Nordic invasion of cross country skiers in Aspen, or parked his car on the street because he hates to valet the Bently. These boasts are displays of his potency and sheer dominance over all other males, and are being made entirely for your benefit. In other words, he's saying: "PICK ME puh-lease."

So never be insulted if a man tries too hard to impress you. Don't confuse his preening for *insecurity*. He's actually paying you an enormous compliment!

Your male is performing an ancient male courtship ritual for your delight, and is so very interested that he's begun flaunting his plumage in a lively display of male prowess and virility. He's letting you know that if you do choose him, you'll be making the right male *selection*. This boastful crowing is no different from a female who tightens her bra straps to present just a little more cleavage. Take it as a feather in your cap and enjoy the show.

If you get bored listening to him sing his own praises, wait till he starts cooing in your ear about how much he loves your gorgeous butt and your beautiful thighs. And then we'll talk. Always beware, however, males flaunting large wads of cash early on. Wealthy men often use money and flash in lieu of real intimacy and heartfelt romance.

Romantic Rule: Remember, men don't have to drop large bills to make you feel like a goddess. They just have to worship you!

Love Songs and Seductive Cooing

Men are visual creatures. Compliments about your outfit and physique are the very first indicators that they're attracted to you. When a man doesn't reassure you with this kind of positive attention, it's a real statement... *about him.* The very least a man can do is say, "Nice hairdo."

MAN FACT: *A man who is attracted to you will naturally want to compliment you. Unless he's been struck mute!*

Compliment Withholders, aka Peckish Mute Warblers. There are some strange birds who stubbornly refuse to give compliments. These men are often *so attracted* to you that they'll try to take you down a notch or two to even out the playing field, aka "negging." by pointing out a flaw in you that you might not even be aware of, because he's making this up!

This lack of generosity is the result of his low self-esteem and indicates a strong tendency to withhold, fight, and always foreshadows trouble. Peckish Mute Warblers like to perch right above you so they can crap on your rainbow, at any time.

The Sweet Mute Warbler. But then there is another type of quiet guy. He's not a bastard, just kinda shy! He simply adores you and is a fabulous guy.

Although he has difficulty singing your praises, Sweet Mutes compensate for this deficiency by lavishing you with lots of loving attention.

Note: These men often make excellent husbands, so stay alert to the differences between the two types of mutes. Choose the sweet, and not the brute!

Professional Songbirds. (See Aviary, The Nightingale.) This smooth talker is *too* adept at the art of the compliment. Listening to a Nightingale sing your praises is delightful, but don't expect too many repeat performances of his arousing arias, because he's often a skilled womanizer, too. And his texts?

Heavenly!

How to Tell Whether You're Being "Wooed" or "Worked"

The key here is in his tone. If the compliments are above the belt, (and his eyeline us above your bra line), as in: "You're so beautiful, gorgeous, amazing, pretty, and smart!" he's singing a lovely tune. If, however, his comments are strictly sexual, these aren't compliments at all, but predatory breeding signals alerting you to the fact that he's preparing to bed you, *and bolt*. Enjoy the serenade if you will, but these aren't love songs my lady. This man is just a lark.

Check out the line my date whispered inyo my ear, just last Saturday night: *"Baby, I want to do bad things to you that I promise you're gonna tlike."*

I have to admit that he was so right!

Always Let Men Sing Your Praises

When I was nineteen, a handsome Brit stopped me and said, "My, you're pretty!" I giggled and shyly looked away. He tipped my chin up with one finger, and said, "When a man gives you a compliment, always look him in the eye and say, "Thank you!"

I turned beet red but did as he bade me. And then he kissed me. I've never forgotten his advice, or that kiss!

Romantic Rule: *Getting paid a compliment is like receiving a gift. It's only polite to respond with easy grace and a thank-you note.*

Etiquette in the Aviary

First-Date Dos and Dont's

If you adhere to smart flirting practices, you'll never get tripped upon first dates ever again, (even when you're in *Louboutin* stilettos).

1. Don't get drunk! Always maintain enough sobriety to assess your date's character. If you start doing Jell-O shots, you may accidentally wind up in the backseat of his Explorer with your skirt around your head. Practice restraint, and don't have more than a drink or two when you're out on a first date. Otherwise, how in the world can you properly assess and observe your bird?

MANHANDLING MANEUVER: *Always stay sober enough to remember how naughty you were the night before!*

2. Don't talk about your personal problems. Therapists get butterflies inside when you talk about your alcoholic relatives or how traumatized you are by the number of germs thriving in public restrooms. The typical male, however, will be horrified. You'll have violated the sacred airspace of "romantic quality time," and these little monologues of strange pain will be as off-putting as offering him a used hankie. If you're prone to making this manhandling mistake, you need a therapist, not a boyfriend. Or a boyfriend who's a therapist.

MANHANDLING MANEUVER: *You already know all about you. Keep your problems to yourself, and find out if he's the right man for you.*

3. Don't be negative about dating. Why should a man pursue someone who isn't happy? It's ineffective manhandling to dump your dating disappointments on Bachelor Number 3. Complaining about how awful dating is just begs the question, "Are you in therapy?"

4. Don't spook your suitor! Don't point out your physical flaws to your lover. Only bring these complaints to people who can actually do something about them, and not to people who are sleeping with you, and who will now be forced to lie to you. Waxers, trainers, manicurists, hairdressers, plastic surgeons, and the staff at *Agent Provacateur*, are among the army of specialists who'll relish discussions about your "problem areas" and dysmorphic body-image. But beware: Once you draw your lover's attention to the little mole that you secretly despise, he'll find it impossible to overlook it, too, *forever*. And forever is a *very* long time.

INTERESTING FACT: Elle McPherson was once asked if there was anything about her physique that she would ever change. "I wish I had better nail beds!" she replied. I've never forgotten it, much to my chagrin. I don't want to think about Elle's nail beds, but there it is . . . lodged in my brain forever, and now in yours, too. Remember: Confidence is sexy!

5. Don't talk badly about your exes. I don't care if he cheated on you with your sister at your Bat Mitzvah, never recite a laundry list of grievances about your exes. This will only make you sound unavailable at best, or worse, *wounded*. Reveal your secrets when you're both on a beach in Hawaii, or better yet, engaged. By then, he'll want to tend to your sniffles. And then you can blow him.

6. Don't cock the gun.

If you're a recovering nymphomaniac or if you've sworn off playing the slots, keep it to yourself for now. Based on my research, anyone who's any fun usually has one or two skeletons in their closet.

> A romance is like an egg.
> When you hold on
> too tightly, it cracks.
> –Lauren Frances

It's unwise, however, to reveal your Achilles' heel to men too soon. When you alert a man about what behaviors won't fly with you, he may sweep a nasty habit or even an addiction right under the rug. If he doesn't run, he'll put on a game face to get you to shag him or, worse, marry him. You'll be stunned when he drains the minibar on your honeymoon and comes home as drunk as a Loon.

MAN FACT: *Men loathe being rejected. It makes them feel bad. Instead, they'd much rather hide any nasty habits they think you'll disapprove of, so that they can seduce you and reject you, instead.*

Remember: It's easier breaking things off on date three than year three! Always let your date reveal his sticky wickets without your interference, to quickly gauge his character.

MANHANDLING MANEUVER: *When you reveal your Achilles' heel too soon, you'll wind up shooting yourself in the the foot.*

7. Don't chase lovebirds!

Never deprive a man the thrill of the chase. Besides, *it's so much fun* being caught! Entice men and then release them is a good rule of thumb. A woman can always feel good about initiating a first teatime date, or the first contact. But once a man has your contact info, he needs to pursue *you.* Allowing men to do the heavy lifting (ie., contacting you and moving your romance forward), will reveal his interest in pursuing you.

The Upside: When you give men space to pursue you, they'll often chase you right up the alter!

MANHANDLING MANEUVER: When you don't chase Lovebirds, they're less likely to fly away!

8. Don't keep squawking. Don't feel pressured to fill up every second with meaningless chatter. If the conversation falls silent for a moment, don't panic, just let it happen. Natural pauses are very sexy, and body language can be so much more powerful than words. Slowly smile at him and breathe. You may be surprised when he blurts out in the middle of a deliciously pregnant pause, "Come here and kiss me!"

MANHANDLING MANEUVER: *Sometimes less conversation is more.*

9. Don't lower the tone. It's easy be pleasant when we're enjoying ourselves, but the true test of character is how we behave when we're terribly bored or, worse, treated shabbily. There's nothing to be gained by suffering through a terrible date. If you're having a gawd-awful time, depart quickly and gracefully, without being rude. When you're itching to leave the Aviary, repair to the powder room, and when you return, do not sit back down, but graciously, say: "Jerome, it was lovely meeting you, but I need to be go home. Thank you so much for coming out to meet me! It was a treat."

Tip: Saying this with a smile *is the key,* and just extend your hand for a quick little shake. Swiftly turn on your heel and depart immediately.

MANHANDLING MANEUVER: *If you're on date number one and aren't having fun, set him free immediately!*

Tip: If he makes any fuss, just tell him you've got cramps.

ten

Bewitching Your Bird

Tools of the Trade

for a Great First Date

The most common mistake that most women tend to make when going on a Manhunt is making an unqualified "impulse buy." Most women tend to be far more skilled at selecting the jeans that they purchase than the men that they're willing to try on for size. The most levelheaded lass will often throw caution to the winds when it comes to qualifying a man for the irreplaceable gift of her time, her heart, and possibly her future!

This is why it's vital to perform rigorous romantic research on your subjects from date one. It will ensure that you don't mistake rabid Prairie Chickens for healthy, available men ever again.

A Properly Handled First Date Should Reveal the Following Intel about your Suitor:

His availability for a relationship right now.

Whether he has problematic "commitment issues."

His attitude about marriage, or whatever kind of relationship that you're looking for!

His relationship history.

His relationship goals.

Your probable odds of future happiness with him.

Did I just hear someone in the back of the room make a crack that there's no way to get that much information from any man on a first date (or during an entire relationship, for that matter)?

You're in for a lovely surprise! When you follow this Man Plan, your date will not only share his innermost secrets with you, he'll *enjoy* himself while he's doing it, too!

Get in the Catbird Seat

You're on your first date and have just ordered a glass of Perrier. "He's so handsome," you think. "I could really like this man!" Instead of getting led astray by unfocused flirting, now is the purrrfect time to collect data with the following playful queries . . .

Q: ***Do you enjoy your work?*** This "innocent" question yields tons of useful information about his financial and emotional stability. If he's proud of his status and accomplishments in the workplace, he'll gladly talk about them in great detail. If he's ashamed, he'll quickly duck the question.

Q: ***Have you recently cared for something that required air to survive?*** Like pets, children, plants, or former spouses. This lets you know if he's dependable and responsible, or if he just likes flying solo.

Q: ***Have you ever had sex with a Republican?*** If you're of a strong political bent, it's always wise to find out if you're on the same team. With such a delightful question, he'll let you know exactly where his allegiance lies and what color stripe he's saluting.

Q: ***Would you like to thumb wrestle?*** This is a fun way to initiate physical contact with men, and gives you oodles of information about a man's competitive nature. Is he a good sport? Does he let you win? Does he hurt you? Is he confident? Does he have nice hands? Are they big? *Now we're talking.*

These questions should be memorized and asked while performing the next man-magnetizing technique. . .

Flying in Formation

When you fly in formation with your Lovebird, he'll think that you're birds of a feather!

1. Play follow the leader. To get in sync with any man, pretend that he's your flock leader and then begin to mirror his physical posture, body movements, and vocal tempo. This is ridiculously easy do while eating an appetizer. *Example:* You're sitting across from each other over drinks. When he leans in, mirror this movement several seconds later by leaning forward. When he settles back into his chair, slowly lean back, too. He'll begin to feel open and relaxed around you.

His inner **GPS (Girl Positioning System)** will be unimpeded; you are wonderful, it says; you're not crowding his airspace one bit. People who are deeply in love automatically do this without giving it conscious thought. They are just "in tune" with each other because they've been having sex all day!

2. Parrot his vocal tempo. Once you're in sync with his move movements, listen to his verbal patterns. If he chirps away excitedly, parrot this upbeat rhythm. If he vocalizes in a more melodious way, answer his call by singing the same seductive tune right back at him.

3. Breathe in unison. Follow his breathing pattern by watching his shoulders rise and fall. Males will respond as if hypnotized when you perform this simple yet powerful tantric yoga practice. Once you play follow the leader for a short while, you'll have set the stage to plunge into the depths of his very soul . . .

4. Ready, aim, fire! By now you're mirroring his posture, his birdsong, and his breathing pattern, but to fully connect with his heart, you must go one step further. While looking deeply into his eyes, slowly inhale. Try to maintain steady eye contact for several seconds longer than you normally would.

 Bonus points! Just break eye contact to compose yourself if this gets too intense. You may even find that you laugh a little. Don't be alarmed if you do. This exercise can make even the most jaded woman blush! He'll find this display of feminine surrender charming. He'll even think he made it happen to you *all by himself.*

He won't notice that you've been mirroring him, but if he does, he'll think that you're both so in sync that you've responded to his call and are naturally following his lead. He won't really know that *he's* been under your spell, and not the other way around. "Hmmm, I wonder if she'll follow me into the bedroom."

Romantic Rule: *Men love to take credit for everything. This is a perfect opportunity to let them!*

Techniques to Enchant Your Man

Breathe slowly and smile softly. Whenever you become nervous, just breathe slowly and deeply, three times in a row. On the first two breaths, look away, but on the third inhalation, raise your eyes to his face, breathe in and out again, and smile softly. This will drive will super-glue his attention, on you.

Draw his attention to you. Any languorous movement done deliberately is fascinating. You might try slowly spreading your napkin on your lap and smoothing it down, or slowly drinking from your glass while looking into his eyes, licking your lips, or twirling your hair around your finger. Gestures like this will captivate him.

Signal your attraction. Communicate your attraction through tiny affectionate gestures, like touching his sleeve, smiling back at him, or brushing up against him accidentally (on purpose). He'll get the message and respond in kind, by taking your hand, and moving closer to you . . . and closer . . .

Note: Flying in formation works in the courtship phase, *and every subsequent phase* of manhandling. If you ever need to have a relationship "talk," this secret maneuver will unlock his heart and make him far less prone to flying off the handle.

Romantic Rule: *Birds of a feather, flock together! You're off to a fantastic start, and a date to remember!*

Pretty Bird

Failure to admire the men who flock to your side is a common mistake of the inexperienced flirter. Whether your bird is a Condor or a Dove, he'll be watching you like a hawk for telltale signs to see if he can satisfy you. It is as if you are a litmus test of his innate masculinity. He'll want to know that you find him desirable. Once you have your fella's full attention, it's a good idea to stroke his fine feathers, by admiring him and singing his praises.

> ADMIRATION: 1. a favorable judgment. 2. feeling aroused by something strange and surprising. 3. "My goodness, you have such big hands. I bet you can open stuck jelly jars with ease!"

MAN FACT: *Men need admiration. It's that simple, people!*

Your date will want to feel capable of filling your bill. If he thinks that it's impossible to impress you, or worse, that you're withholding your approval, he'll flee. He'll want a woman who approves of him and admires him, and who can blame him? This could be why older men prefer to date nineteen-year-olds, but it's only a theory.

MAN FACT: *Men want to be with women who are smart enough to see the best in them.*

If you're a handful (strong, smart, and sassy), your bird will be on high alert to see if he can make you happy. The wise Manhandler makes it her business to stroke the nervous bird to counteract this tendency. When you learn the art of validating men, they'll feel encouraged, and capable of satisfying you.

Tip: Failure to admire men is the single biggest reason women don't get asked out on Date Number Two!

Make Him Puff Out His Chest

A man loves nothing better than being praised. Don't blow smoke up his tail. Just parrot back something positive that he's been twittering away about during the course of your conversation.

Love Script to make him puff out his chest:

For the man who is trying to impress you with his mental heft:
    "You're so smart. I love a man with a big brain."
    "What inspired you to study particle physics?"
    "Tell me, George, what can I do about global warming?"

For the wild man artist:
    "You're so intriguing. Tell me more about (whatever he's whipping up in the studio). I'm fascinated."

For the blue-collar, macho regular Joe:
    "I am so sick of wimpy guys!"
    "Ooh, can you help? The top is stuck on this ketchup bottle."

For the single, divorced father who has fought to retain custody of his kids:
    "You have such a great values system."
    "How is his soccer team doing this year?"

For the A-type success monger who has rattled off a long list of his accomplishments:
    "What an alpha male!"
    "I find you sooooo inspiring."

For the guy who's nervous and shy:
    "I feel wonderful right now! It's so nice being here with you."

For the grad student who's working two jobs, too:
    "What commitment and stamina. I love that kind of drive in a man! You must be an animal in the bedroom." Wink.

For the man who is flashing his cash:
    "I feel so taken care of tonight. What a treat. Thank you!"

For the man who's trying to seduce you:
    "I feel so sexy around you."
    "You make me want to do terrible things!"
    "Purrrr."

Don't do this: I was once on a date with a man, and said, "You dress like a dad.

"Well, I am a dad," he said.

"Yes," I replied, "but you're not my dad!"

Romantic Rule: *Always remember to thank your date for dinner DURING your date. Do not send him a text message afterwards! It'll botch your "experiment." If he wants to see you again, he'll call you. No exceptions!*

How to Predict His Lovemaking Style over Dinner

`Observe his body language!`

• If he touches you often, he's the **reassuring type.**

• If you touches you too much, he's the **invasive type.**

• If he places his hand on the small of your back, **he's a caretaker.**

• If he's nervous and flighty, he's **nervous and flighty.**

• If his shoulders are hunched in a protective defensive stance, **he's inaccessible.**

• If his body is open and relaxed, **he's inviting.**

• If he sprawls, **he's confident.**

• If he holds his limbs in a controlled way, **he's intense.**

• If he takes your hand, or kisses it, he's **romantic and tender.**

• If he takes confident control of the waiter while ordering for you, **he's sexy!**

eleven

Date Interrogation

Men are like sweaters. Once you remove the
tags, they're so much harder to return.

—Lauren Frances

Beware The Goose
Who Lays the Golden Egg
(aka The Secret Male Lemon Law Disclaimer)

There's a well-kept secret about men that you may not know, but once you do, it's guaranteed to save you more heartache than a six-barrel shotgun.

MAN FACT: *Men will tell you almost anything on the first two dates and then clam up for the next two years.*

After that, it will take a team of wild horses to drag him to therapy to talk about his "relationship issues." *(And aren't we just sick of that?)* That's why the best time to get information out of a man is right at the beginning of your courtship. If you listen carefully, men tell you everything you need to know about them, including whether they're worthy of you. So always take this golden opportunity to learn the inner secrets of your new feathered friend.

Now, men have an innate sense of honor, but they aren't stupid. No one knows their faults better than they do, so they've devised an ingenious strategy to facilitate the propagation of the species and maintain their personal integrity, *no matter what kind crazymakers or deviants they are..*

MAN FACT: *While men are strutting their stuff, they'll also lay a little "golden egg" of valuable intel.*

It'll whip right by you if you're not listening for it, but if you are, it'll surely come. While he prattles on about his stock portfolio or boasts of his world travels, your date will let slip exactly what's wrong with him in the relationship department.

The Secret Disclaimer is always hidden in the fine print. It will be only a sentence or two, or even a little monologue if you're lucky. But once he lets it slip, he'll camouflage it under such a magnificent display of fine feathers you'll have a hard time spotting the 666 branded right in the middle of his beautiful chest.

MAN FACT: *The Secret Male Lemon Law Disclaimer is often passed off as a joke.*

Because it's so tiny in comparison with all of his male posturing, the disclaimer may seem totally inconsequential at the time. Besides, no woman in her right mind would be so flagrantly off-putting if she actually liked someone!

> *"I'm a pervert," says he.*
> *"How funny!" thinks she.*

She'll usually dismiss it entirely, until three years later, when she sits bolt upright in the middle of the night and finally puts it all together. *He told her on their first date that he was cheating on his mistress!* She laughed right along with him at the time because she thought it was a joke, and now he's having sex with the dog walker.

LEMON LAW DISCALIMERS: *These gems of invaluable information often make sense only in hindsight, after three months, or three years, of wasted time and effort.*

And to top it all off, he'll think that he was a good guy for warning you about his foibles. And if you bitch about it to him later, he'll remind you that he told you from date one that he was still sleeping with his ex or that his last relationship was a polyamorous thruple. You see, once a man lays the golden egg, he's no longer responsible for it. *You are.* When you get hurt, it's your problem, because he straight up let you know, and you went right ahead and got involved with him anyway. You silently agreed to his terms; now he gets off scot-free and guilt free, too.

Actual "Lemon Law Disclaimers" I've Heard on First Dates

"Why get married? You just lose half your shit!"

"People think I'm terrible for not being married, but at least I'm not cheating on my wife."

"I've never been in love."

"I only have time to date once or twice a month."

"My fiancée cheated on me with a twenty-two-year-old. I have a very short fuse now."

"My wife said she doesn't love me anymore. Why doesn't she love me?

"The last girl I dated was eighteen."

"My ex-wife hates me."

"My ex-girlfriend was crazy! I've been single ever since."

"My longest relationship was seven months."

(Seven months?!) Even I couldn't pretend that I hadn't heard that.

Amazingly, these lemons were all slipped into conversations during romantic dinners, in fabulous restaurants, while my dates collectively managed to boast about a $7 million home on Malibu beachfront property, legendary fame, 21 Emmy's, a star on Hollywood Boulevard, 15 gold records, a cock just shy of Tommy Lee's, 350 avocado trees, tennis courts, an IQ of 156, a bankroll north of $100 mill.

They also offered to take me to Paris *(merci)*, Italy, Spain *(olé)*, Scotland (did accept this offer), London (this one, too), the spa (yup), Turkey, Amsterdam (don't like herring), Ojai (uh-huh), Vegas (hit the jackpot at the slots!*)*, Puerto Vallarta (had fun), the Caribbean . . .

All right, I'm a sucker for a fabulous trip. One promised to give me the most fabulous orgasms on earth (true) . . . and on and on.

But remember the lemons? They make even the sweetest moments a little sour, the hottest guys become unattractive, and the richest men seem like paupers.

MAN FACT: *Now nobody's perfect, but some men are definitely more perfect than others.*

So don't kill the goose who lays the golden egg . . . thank him for it. He just saved you a lot of time and aggravation. Learn the secrets of the men who would be king of your emotional castle by carefully listening to them, and *believing* them.

Romantic Rule: *Everyone has problems. You just need to find someone who has problems you can live with.*

Mandatory Homework
After Every First Date

Hop into bed, pull out the Lovebirds' Field Notes *(See page 77)*, and fill in your new specimen's profile without delay. Make sure to record any Lemon Law Findings. Any little "Hmm, that was odd" or "I'm not sure what he meant when he said ____", count as placeholders for your future queries into his charachter, too.

If you're ridiculously attracted to him or impressed with his fine feathers, always share his Secret Male Lemon Law Disclaimer with a trusted member of your Mantrap Pack.

That way, if you wind up slipping into a sex coma, your pal can give you some perspective on your fledgling romance (*he's a professional poker player, you nitwit!*). This will help keep you abreast of your findings, and keep your head out of the clouds and your feet on the ground.

Make Him Sing Like a Canary

Some men are cagier than others. The harder it is to get a confession out of your subject, the more he usually has to tell. If your bird doesn't open up easily, you'll want to make him *reveal* his secret past by slipping him some truth serum while you're having drinks. To make him sing like a canary, ask my **Heartache Prevention Questions:** "So, Clark, when was the last time you were in love?" Or "How long have you been single?" before you ever meet him, (on the telephone). Asking Heartache Prevention Questions in an offhanded way will make any man talk a blue streak, so pay very close attention to their responses.

Romantic Rule: *This is like putting a turban on your head, and more effective than calling the psychic network, because you'll get a little preview about how he'll talk about the both of you, right after you break up!*

This is the one and only time you can ask such a loaded question without it being "heavy" because you can't possibly take the answer to this question personally . . . yet. You'll be amazed to discover how men flap their jaws with ease about deep emotional problems on a first date with total strangers. And for the women who've only been privy to this type of soul-bearing honesty from men during tearful breakups, I promise that you will be stunned.

When you ask the Heartache Prevention Question, men will tell you exactly how they feel about marriage, often revealing whether they're financially stable, are adamantly or morally opposed to the state of matrimony itself, or are having too much fun playing the field to even think about settling down. They'll also divulge the status of prior marriages and custody arrangements and stupidly confess about their current roster of out-of-town girlfriends as well. I am so not kidding.

Tip: Listen very carefully to how he talks about his exes and be on the lookout for any pet 'relationship theories.' He might tell you, for example, that "love doesn't really exist" or that all of his relationships "end up the same way . . . 'in court.'"

Congratulations! You have thoroughly broken your subject. He has just revealed his inner 'romantic guidance system.' It's what he believes to be true about relationships and love, *and it isn't going to change.* Most people just repeat their mating patterns over and over again with somebody new, and that could mean you. If he's given you troubling information, it will steer all of his relationships in the same direction . . . south. This is hard to reprogram without divine intervention—or intense therapy. Or a hard smack on the noggin.

So when he starts talking, listen up! You've hit the jackpot. The last time I administered verbal truth serum, my date leaned in and said: "I told you my ex just moved to Dallas with my seven year old son, didn't I? I'm suing her for alimony. She's loaded!"

I suddenly got a "splitting headache" and quickly called it a night!

MAN FACT: *If he says he says every woman he's been with is psycho, remember that he's the one that picked 'em!*

When you hear information like this, *believe him.* The next question to ask is "Have you gone to therapy for that?"

If he says yes, ask him if it's *working.*

If It Walks Like a Duck . . .

Q: *If a man reveals that he was chronically unfaithful to his wife, has "anger issues" but he's working on them" or has vowed to never remarry . . .*

A: He is not your future husband.

MAN FACT: *If it walks like a duck and talks like a duck . . . he's a not gonna get lucky!*

You are Now Dating Like an International Spy . . .

If you've followed my instructions thus far, you'll have thoroughly bewitched your Lovebird, and he'll have revealed his innermost secrets to you. He'll feel so connected to you that he'll have lowered his guard, dropped the drawbridge, and invited you right into the castle of his inner self.

The tiny questions you ask, the way you mirror his body movements,the attention and validation you give him—these will be like a narcotic to him. Your date will have become very open, intimate, and even, gasp, *vulnerable.*

But heed this warning: Don't get too comfortable and jump right in and start telling your war stories, too, or your entire evening will turn into a therapy session.

Romantic Rule:: *Don't become his therapist! When your subject opens up, actively listen.*

Nod your head sympathetically and say:

"Ahhhh."

"Hmmm . . . I get it."

"Wow, you must be strong to have survived that."

"That must have been soooo difficult."

"You seem so well adjusted. Did you go to therapy for that?"

"Waiter, check please!

Then go home, strip off your gloves, and hop right in the tub.

Congratulations on a job well done!

twelve

Clay Pigeons

In truth, you don't need a million men, just a fun flock of runners-up, until a true Lovebird comes in for a landing. Sadly, there's no way to play the field without incurring dating disappointments and some downright failures. This fact won't be quite as daunting once you learn how to swiftly terminate a failed romantic experiment. This chapter gives you all the ammo you need to shoot down pesky lame ducks.

How to Handle Turbulence

You're both having a great time, when BAM! All of a sudden you hit a bad patch and you find yourself gripping your seat.

Don't panic. Turbulence is always a cue to excuse yourself and go take a quick "date-break" in the nearest powder room. Take a breath of fresh air and slowly reapply your lip gloss. After a little touch-up, you may come back completely refreshed and find that your date's ruffled feathers have smoothed down, too. But if turbulence continues for more than several minutes (three), simply part ways. You're in for a very bumpy ride!

Romantic Rule: Don't try to work things out if you hit an extended rough patch with a new suitor, too soon. Just quickly deplane!

True Story: Once, while on a terrible date, my aunt Pat excused herself from the table, slipped the waiter a $10 bill, and said, "Tell the man in the corner booth that I'm leaving and that I'm never coming back!"

Don't you love that?

Terrible Turbulence
Always Shoot a Man Down If:

• Has the nerve to check out other women , or flirts with them in front of you.
• He's in a bad mood.
• He's too sexually forward.
• He's disrespectful or insults you.
• He makes you feel crappy, or in any way makes you feel unhapppy.

• Is STILL heartbroken about an ex.
• He's drunk!
• He picks a fight with you, or the waiter, valet car parker, or ex-wife on the phone.
•You start arguing about politics
•Doesn't look like his pix

Tell these Turkeys to buzz off

Romantic Rule: Never stay in the room, or get into a car with a man you barely know, (ever!) who's surly, drunk, or in a foul mood.

Was He "Winging It?"

• wants to meet for a drink after his workout because he's already eaten, and you've made a dinner plan, **he's cheap.**

• asks you in a whiny voice, "What would you like to do?" and has nothing fun to suggest, he's a lazy whiner. (Exceptions: If he's new to your part of town, or expending the effort to meet you by traveling a great distance. Then suggest away!

• makes out with you, vanishes, and reappears several weeks later, he's just a **booty-call.**

• wants you to meet him somewhere very low-key, or just at your apartment, he's possibly **very married. Cyber sleuth him!**

• takes you to the mall or a fast-food restaurant and says he's keeping the date "real," **he's broke.** Or **very rich** and trying to keep that on the DL.

• takes you to special places, but suddenly stops doing it, **you're demoted.**

• doesn't put any thought or effort into figuring out how to spend quality time with you, aka not investing in your relationship, he's a **nitwit.**

• only expends an effort of the sexual kind, **he's not your husband!**

The Problem with Being "Nice"

Rejecting unsuitable suitors is just awkward. And this the real reason why so many women dread dating. They get in trouble because they're way "too nice." They don't like hurting anyone's feelings, and often wind up in a whole heap of (avoidable) trouble.

Fortunately, the art of releasing men back into the wilds is easy to do, with some magic phrases. But first, let's find out if you've been falling into a big dating trap.

Are you "Too Darned Nice?"

Nice girls don't know how to "drop men from the flock" that they don't want to see.

Nice girls agree to dates they shouldn't really be on, and they often say yes, and just "people-please"

Nice girls don't listen to their feelings (and intuition), and agree to first or second dates with wing-nuts.

Nice girls let men take off condoms or go undercovers, when they'd rather say, *"No thanks, Bud! I'm allergic to nuts."*

Nice girls don't set limits when men step outta line.

Nice girls don't say, *"Hasta la vista!" "Finito"* and *"There won't be a 'next time.'"*

Romantic Rule: If he's not the One, he's just blocking traffic!

And let's get you some chops . . .

Shoot 'Em Down with "The Dear John Phoner"

How to Break Up Via Text or Phonecall

You need to learn how to say, "NO" to find a man that's a "YES!" And it's going to be easier than you think, if you just read the words I've written out for you as a Lovescript to pleasantly say "Nyet! Next."

1: When you need to cut a man loose, end the date as soon as humanly possible and extend your right hand for a quick little shake. Period. End.
2: If he calls and tries to bore you to tears again, simply break the bad news to him with the Dear John Phoner, or text.

The Dear John Phoner protects you from any angry outbursts of temper and has other added benefits: no awkward partings, uncomfortable car rides, or indigestion after dining.

Romantic Rule: If you haven't gone "undercover" with a man, it's perfectly fine to just send a Dear John text!

Instead of meeting him in person (aka. DRAMA), give him the bad news quickly in the brief phone call or text. And the upside? He'll get the message, and henceforth leave you alone. This is fine to do if you've gone on several dates, or even a few.

Tip: And if men have been bastards, no matter how long you've been dating, you don't need to see 'em in person, at all!

Love Script for "The Dear John Phoner"

MAN FACT: *Being rejected at distance (via phone or text) is far less humiliating than being shot down at close range. It allows men to save face, and lick their wounds in private.*

When you need to nix a suitor, say or text the following Lovescript in a pleasant but decisive way; "It was great meeting you, Rick, but I'm just not feeling that little "Click." But I really appreciate you making the time for us both to have met!"

You'll be delighted to discover that you are rewarded for your candor with a *"Thanks for letting me know!"* kind of text.

But ff he asks the dreaded "Why?" don't be specific!

Tip: Men are like attorneys. They'll start asking for specifics so that they can outwit you and get you to agree to just one more date, if they really like you. Don't give men a reason to start cross-examine you, and start to explain why.

Or he might lob you the insidious; "Can't we just be friends?" request, as a last ditch try. Shut this down. If you're single and want to find a lovebird, you don't have that kind of time.

Just say, "It's just a gut feeling, and I promised myself after my last breakup to *always* trust it. It was a disaster! But I do wish you well!" And then hop off the line!

Always remember: No one can argue with that still, small voice, inside of you. It's invulnerable to attack.

Even in Milan.

Irritating and Intrusive Birdcalls

"No" is a complete sentence. If a man repeatedly calls after you've told him that you don't want to see him, screen his calls and don't ever return them again. You have set a boundary, and the boundary is NO. If you allow him to bully or wheedle his way back in, you'll have no one but yourself to blame. If you shut the little pecker out, he'll eventually tire of this game and move on.

Romantic Rule: *You must learn how to say ,"NO!" if you want to say, "Hell yes!" to the right man. Reject (un)romantic detours!*

Is He Bowing Out?

When you really like someone, and he doesn't really return your feelings, it stings! But if he didn't respond to your hot ass, then you definitely do not need to see *his.*

If he doesn't compliment you . . .

If he doesn't walk you to your door . . .

If he doesn't say he had a great time . . .

If he doesn't try to touch you . . .

If he doesn't talk about future plans . . .

If he says, "I'll call you" without any enthusiasm . . .

If he doesn't try and kiss you good-bye . . .

If he says, "Thanks for coming out. It was nice to meet you"

If he says,"Let's stay in touch". . .

If he peels away before you get safely into your Uber, or peels out befoe you're in your front door . . .

         . . . he's probably bowing out.

He was just a Clay Pigeon. Simply write him off as failed research. Don't bother wasting your time trying to figure out why he doesn't want to pursue you. You can never accurately figure out why things don't click with strange birds that you barely know.

I subscribe to the old adage "Their rejection is God's protection." If you have to make up a story about why he's bowing out, it's always better to make up one that makes you feel better, instead of one designed for self torture! This kind of date replay can make a woman want to hide under her covers and give up on men altogether if it's indulged in too often. It's a very bad habit to persist in, and even worse than nail biting.

Instead, why not try this on for size? He was terribly attracted to you but suspected you'd have a zero-tolerance policy about his erectile dysfunction. Better, right?

I knew the truth would set you free!

Romantic Rule: *Don't turn the gun on yourself! Always shoot down Clay Pigeons.*

thirteen

Lovebird's Field Notes

It is essential to take thorough field notes of your romantic research. Use the handy checklist below to identify and catalog the different types of birds that you've lured to your side. If you've been observant, you'll have gleaned important clues about which members of your flock are serious contenders for mating purposes, just naughty playthings, or men to set free immediately!

Subject:

His name / Username:

Phone Number / IG Handle:

Species:

Subspecies:

Date Assessment

Arrival time:

Location of date:

Did he make reservations?

Do you have any reservations about him?

Conversational skills:

Courtesy level:

Date attentiveness:

Generous or cheap?

His Investment: Attention, Cash, Flash, Enthusiasm?

Birdsong and compliments?

Departure: (Romantic, Sexual, Awkward, or Distant?)

Good-night kiss? Hot or not?

Did he try to rebook you?

Did he make you feel special? How?

On cloud 9? Smooth sailing?

Was it entertaining? How?

Would have rather done laundry?

Was there any turbulence?

Temperament

Cooing Dove: ....

Wounded Bird: ....

Peckish and Irritable: ....

Fighting Cock: ....

Predatory Raptor: ....

Nesting and relaxed: ....

Preening Peacock: ....

Cockfighting Peckerhead: ....

Your Attraction Level (Rate from 1-10)

Sexual chemistry: ....

His brainpower: ....

His lifestyle: ....

His personality: ....

Grooming: ....

His aroma: ....

Hi bod: ....

His values: ....

Character Assessment

Was he positive about life and love?

Any red flags?

Any Lemon Drops or Disclaimers?

Unusual traits or habits?

Is he unresolved about any past relationships?

Status of past relationships: (Fighting, Enmeshed, Wounded? Free and clear?)

Would you leave a child in his care?

What is his "mission" in life?

Does he do charity work?

Is he a member of a spiritual community?

Does he have pets?

Plants?

Life Stage

What live stage is he in? (Juvenile, Breeding, or Nesting)

What are his relationship goals?

Did he state any sexual preferences? (Note: This is a "thing" if he brings it up before or during a first date!)

Does he have children?

How involved is he with their care?

Does he feel like a success? In what aspects of his life?

Is He Socialized?

Any displays of aggression?

Road rage, sharp tongue, rudeness to you or others?

Did he offend you in any way?

Was he too sexually aggressive?

Did he put you on the defensive?

Did he check out other women?

Did he try to make you jealous?

His relationship history: Did he have happy and healthy relationships or divulge broken and unhappy partnerships and angry exes?

Vocalizing Skills and Conversational Style

Flowing

Road rage, sharp tongue, rudeness to you or others?

Seemed bored

Sparkling

Snappy

Fun

Attentive

Engaged

Like pulling teeth

Classification

Is he an early bird or a night owl?

Ready for nesting

Predatory Raptor

Juvenile male?

Snowy Owl?

Was he a Lame Duck?

Is he a fledgling (IE. too young, just got out of rehab, recently separated, or unemployed?)

Conclusions

Significant findings:

Date assessment:

Your comfort level:

Your attraction level:

Your intuitive "hunch" or romantic "prediction"

Drop from your flock? Or is he a keeper?!

His Date Rating:

The 5 Star Date Rating System

For date-classification purposes, use this rating system to put Lovebirds in the right pecking order!

• He's a keeper! Give him five stars. *****

• If you're dating, and he doesn't return a text or a call by the very next day, he loses 2 stars!
• If he drops below 1 star, he's on date probation! Accept other dates, and put hm on simmer!
• Now remember, not everybody starts out with five stars. If you're not really sure if you're attracted to him, he can start out with only three stars and work his way up! Give him at leat 3 dates if you are compatible in other very imortannt ways, and do the "Kiss Test" before he's dismissed!

Important Tip: Get X-Ray Vision: If you don't like his outfit, hair gel, or cologne, his is not a good reason to dismiss suitors You can always take thise kinds of men shopping! Men appreciate it, and you'll get a gold star from HIM! And then they'll often wind up taking YOU ring shopping! (Tons of my married clients have followed this advice, right up the altar

Happy hunting, Sister!

Men and women both want to get each other on their knees, but for very different reasons!

–Lauren Frances

mating
part ii

Shopping for men is exactly like . . . shopping!

–Lauren Frances

fourteen

Bird Selection

Man selection should follow the same guidelines as successful pet selection. Choose a man who possesses an even-keeled and loving temperament. He should be cooperative, reasonable, well-mannered, and easy to train. Housebroken would be nice, too. But if a man requires excessive punishment, attention, and emotional energy, it's probably unwise to keep your pet . . . I mean, man.

Go for the domesticated lovebird. When selecting the right male for you, it's always a boon if he's already been domesticated. Men who've been in successful long-term relationships tend to fall into this category. These men are like self-walking dogs! The upside for the already housebroken male is obvious. He'll grab some Midol for you while he's out buying beer and has mastered the difficult phrase "No problem," and the harder "Yes dear." But he'll still throw wet towels on your silk duvet.

Always consider the predomesticated male. This man was raised by a loving single mother. Not only is he pre trained, he keeps house far better than you and knows about secret cleaning techniques like bleaching the sink! *The downside:* Your towel folding methods may be held up to ridicule. The predomesticated male makes for an incredibly well-trained and sensitive partner, unless he has "issues" with Mom. Then he's virtually untenable and is probably better left outdoors.

The garden-variety wild birdman. Unwilling to modify his behavior for the indoors, the wild birdman lives under the radar and flies above the law—Female Law, that is—as in socks in the hamper and no tequila after dawn. He rips through your house like a tornado.

He gets miffed if he feels he's been criticized. Helpful comments like "You should've made a left at that stop sign, babe" can make this sensitive bird fly into a snit! Many women agree that the wild birdman is the most common species of male around. Once you learn how to manhandle him, however (see Part Three), you may discover he makes quite a delightful partner.

Beware the previously owned problem bird. Sometimes even the most adorable man exhibits antisocial behavior after a small "settling in" period. He suddenly becomes cocky, rude, and uncooperative or, worse, he transforms into a world-class screamer or nitpicking fussbudget. This change in temperament occurs the second he thinks he's got his talons wrapped right around your little finger. In order for him to be a tolerable housemate, you'll need to take this bird down a notch or two and give him an Altitude Adjustment. (*See* Give Him an Altitude Adjustment, page 183.)

Predatory Raptors

Once upon a time there was a very bored but beautiful princess . . .

You hyperventilate as he artfully kisses you, bites your neck, and tells you everything he already knows that you want to hear. He will make you his, and his alone. He's hell-bent on it. This usually won't take very long, maybe only a couple of weeks of intense phone calling, texting, and sweet-talking.

But once you get hooked on his attention, he suddenly disappears, leaving you all alone in your (now) drafty turret, peering out of tiny windows and wondering where he went. You fervently pray for his speedy return; in distress, you consult the court's fortune tellers for answers.

"What happened? Did I say something wrong? Did I hurt his feelings?" you ask your girlfriends in a panic.

Of course you didn't! He just knew how to work you into a state of intense *romantic hopefulness*.

You're shocked when you figure out what was behind the big hard on he used to knock you off balance with. He was just jousting! You didn't realize he was in this for sport, and are stunned to find that you were put on a pedestal only to be knocked on your ass. Still, you can't stop thinking about him, or talking about him, and wondering where he went. And when he's coming back. You feel a little crazy. You're now plagued with positively torturous medieval longing.

The Queen noticed that Lancelot avoided her now and rode away from Camelot on every quest that was offered. She sent for him and said: "Lance, I see and feel daily that your love for me grows less, and you ride ever to help damsels in distress. Have you perhaps found one who is dearer to your heart than I?"

You'll have to wait more than a little while for Lance-a-lots to return. These types of men are busy. So many women to bone, so little time! Maybe that's why he was in such a rush after all. Then, miraculously, he calls (*See* Wild Blue Yonder Caller, page 152.) You're elated! He gives you some lame excuse about why he couldn't call you: "*An infestation of rats overran the castle.*" "*A bunch of us feudal lords went on a snowboarding trip. The powder was perfect.*"

You accept his lack of apology immediately because he has managed to make you feel *really* insecure. You didn't like being tossed aside and want to be lovingly placed back where you know you deserve to be. If not up on a pedestal, then any old chair will do. Oh, who are we kidding; you'll be on your knees the next time you see him!

Q: **What happened?**

A: By building up your expectations and then dashing them just as fast, the Predatory Raptor knocks you off center and now has the upper hand. This is a manipulation, and he knows it. BEWARE!! The Predatory Raptor is no Lovebird, my lady. If he were, he wouldn't have loved you and left you holding the emotional bag.

Romantic Rule:: *If you're spending a lot of time wondering what's happening, he's probably wandering!*

Lesson: We don't want men we have to contact on the astral plane. We want men we can actually talk to, and who show up on Friday night to take us out for sushi.

MAN FACT: *Be suspicious of men who try to rush into (or out of) anything too soon, like a storybook romance or your pantaloons*

The Wounded Bird
(aka The Instant Boyfriend)

The Instant Boyfriend starts out being quite charming . . . for two or three dates. Then he'll try to control you with displays of immediate and intense possessiveness. Setting up expectations of future Us-ness, he begins his onslaught by calling you every day, sometimes multiple times a day. *Problem:* You've only been dating one week! He's actually doing this as a form of surveillance to keep tabs on you, and create a No-Fly Zone for other incoming males. This is a passive way of locking you in his little tower, and the telephone is his wrought-iron key.

The Wounded Bird has "Broken Wing Syndrome." This display of (faux) vulnerability is actually a powerful technique he uses to excuse his suspicious and needy behavior.

Translation: I was cheated on by my last girlfriend so I'm going to drive you crazy by crowding you and checking up on you in ways that you can't even imagine.

The Wounded Bird is manipulative. Instant Boyfriends also sometimes turn into instant stalkers. What starts out as "cute" often becomes oppressive, smothering, and controlling.

Here's a perfet example from my client Courtney. . .

Case Study: The Wounded Bird

Courtney, 31, model/waitress & Frank, 42 therapist

"I met Frank at work. He was cute so I gave him my number. He immediately started calling every day and wanting to speak every night. He said his ex-wife cheated on him with a twenty-two-year old. He still seemed really angry about it. We had only gone on three dates when he started saying things like *"Do you miss me?"* I wasn't quite sure how to respond, so I played along.

One night, I didn't return a message he'd left. I was tired, and after all, we'd only been dating for a week and a half! He wasn't really my boyfriend yet. He gave me a very hard time about it, grilling me about why I didn't want to speak to him. I told him several times that I was just tired after a long night's work. Just talking to him started feeling like a lot of work!

In the beginning, he seemed so interested in my life, unlike a lot of other guys. He would ask questions in such a nice way that I'd tell him everything.

"So what did you do today, where were you? Did you have fun? Who were you hanging out with? Were there any guys there? Did you talk to any of them?" That's when I realized he was actually quizzing me to keep tabs on me! I told him I wanted to stop seeing him, and he got very angry about it. **Dating this man felt like joining a cult.** I finally stopped taking his calls, but it took him awhile to get the message."

Lesson: If you're feeling smothered or controlled as quickly as all that, drop him in two seconds flat.

Marrying Men and Bachelors

There are only two kinds of men in this world, marrying men and bachelors. Marrying men *like* being in relationships with women. In fact, they need them. Now, "need" isn't the dirty word we've been taught to revile, because in truth, men only marry the women they need. Otherwise, they'd just keep burning through women and replacing them with different models . . . who sometimes are models.

Whoops! Allow me to refocus.

Marrying men prefer having a special someone to call every day. The *same* someone. These men are often categorized as serial monogamists, but this makes them sound like criminals. This is so unfair because, in truth, they are wonderful!

MAN FACT: *Men who are emotionally available show up immediately. They don't have dramatic problems that prevent them from moving a relationship forward.*

A guy prime for the plucking is direct, makes his intentions clear, and usually proposes within six months to one year. He's landed that big job, is ready to buy that house, and has finally stopped wanting to have sex with his ex. He feels good about himself, but hopefully not *too* good. Actually, it would be best if he felt a tad insecure . . . and vulnerable enough to be grateful that God sent him another chance at love . . . in the form of *you.*

Men Prime for the Plucking . . .

• Feel incomplete being single.

• Move from one serious relationship to the next.

• Say things like "I'm looking to get married" with the ease of a man saying, "My company is looking for a receptionist."

• Use the words *we, us* and *when.*

• Bring up the subject of marriage, family, and commitment on their own, unflinchingly, and without prodding.

• Ask qualifying questions like *"What was your last relationship like?"* or blurts out things like, *"I can't believe you're not married yet!"*

You can relax around such a man because he's taking care of business, which means you can quite happily take care of his bizness!

Cocks of the Walk
(aka the Hardened Bachelor)

And then there are bachelors. They can take women or leave them, and so often do. Because they have poor relationship skills, bachelors become masters of seduction or they'd *never* get laid.

The Hardened Bachelor has an idealized fantasy that no mortal woman can live up to, or would want to. He'll treat you like a goddess and worship at your shrine for an intoxicating three weeks to three months, but beware! He'll become strangely repulsed by your allergy to dust and get turned off when he discovers that you're human. If you think these men have hearts of stone, though, you're wrong. The Hardened Bachelor is *deeply in love...* with himself.

Note: This man is selfish except when it comes to sex. And that's where you come in. Right through the little zippered door!

MAN FACT: *The bachelor needs only one thing from women: sex. And he gets this for free from most women without any kind of commitment at all, maybe just for the price of one dinner!*

The Hardened Bachelor has unreasonable needs for "space" that no woman can withstand and are meant to drive her away. His rigid boundaries ensure that you'll remain too distant for real intimacy/expectation to occur. As soon as he feels he's being emotionally hemmed in, he *panics.* This is one reason why this type of man prefers dating very young women. He knows that they probably aren't ready for marriage and won't pressure him in any way that he can't easily handle. Besides, young girls look fantastic in a thong and just want to party! And so, I might add, does he.

MAN FACT: *Hardened Bachelors feel that women are to be used for their pleasure and then replaced, kind of like batteries.*

Are you disposable? I don't think so!

Identifying Characteristics of
The Hardened Bachelor

• Is still traumatized from a twisted relationship deep in his past—with Mommy or an ex—that even therapy can't undo.

• Makes wisecracks about how "unhappy" all of his happily married friends are.

• Uses the words *me, mine* and *maybe.*

• If he was married, he definitely cheated! and
• Goes through women like truckers guzzling coffee at a rest stop.

A Hardened Bachelor Only
Marries When . . .

A. He "accidentally" knocks up a twenty-two-year-old (she plans this) and then he'll try to do the right thing. But he'll hate family life, cheat on her, blame her for it, leave her, and then bitch about it for the next seventeen years.

B. Some life-changing event occurs and he has a total change of relationship perspective. This could look like turning fifty, having a near death experience (ball cancer), or erectile dysfunction. His lifestyle now seems a tad shallow and self-centered, even to him, and he suddenly longs for, dare I say it, family life. So he sets about procuring a young wife who'll look hot in a nurse's uniform while pushing his wheelchair in his golden years.

C. He runs across a woman who has such incredible self-esteem that she refuses to sell herself out. She sets a standard that he'll need to rise to if he wants to bed her (*See* Amal Clooney). This will stun him, irritate him, and titillate him into evolving into a better man, but this kind of transformation is so rare that it's almost not worth mentioning.

BEWARE: If a Hardened Bachelor actually lets his guard down long enough to fall in love with you, he'll be virtually tool-free when it comes to working on a real relationship. He's often immature, petty, and prone to terrible fits of jealousy, and he comes with a slew of totally dysfunctional behaviors. You'll soon discover that the only thing that he's learned to work out with a woman is located in his BVD's!

The Dominant Cocks of the Walk
Formerly known as
"George Clooney Syndrome"

He's in his forties and is still so fine that he feels no pressure to settle down. The ladies love him, his career is on fire, and there is no end of T&A in sight. He can date in every age range and bed whomever he wants because he's charismatic, handsome, and, well . . . *him.* He's a master at making women feel really, really special because he loves them. One at a time, or in delightful combinations of twos and threes!

These men aren't monogamous. They don't have to be. Besides, what's a bonbon or two when you've been offered the whole damn box?

Men with George Clooney Syndrome fly in tight flocks composed of other rich, sexy, and equally unavailable males. Their long-term primary relationships are often with one another. But they are available to women for sex and fun, or long-term, non-exclusive sexual arrangements, and sometimes high-profile marriages riddled with extra marital liaisons.

Unless you're a soaring starlet (or Amal Clooney), you'll find this man impossible to nest with. These guys won't slow down or become eligible for marriage until they hit their mid to late fifties, and by then, who wants 'em? (Okay, we all still do, but let's try to make great choices moving forward!)

WARNING: These swinging bachelor's are perfect for awesome rocking chair memories. It's thrilling to be with them, but you may get a little dizzy from the intense ups and downs. So take it lying down! Enjoy the ride, but don't say I didn't warn you when it comes to its abrupt, inevitable, and heart-wrenching end.

Yeah, I know . . . that's why God made girlfriends.

fifteen

Don't Count Your Chickens Before They Hatch!

The Heartache Prevention Handbook

Girls love to jump to romantic conclusions. This phenomenon usually starts occurring in junior high, when they write a boy's name all over their biology homework with small hearts over the i's. Here's a page of my own seventh-grade handiwork:

David Boyd
D. Boyd
Mrs. David Boyd.
Mr. and Mrs. David & Lauren Boyd
Lauren Boyd . . .
mmmmmmmmmmm

All right. I never even kissed David Boyd. But I did spend many a dreamy hour in seventh grade very much married to him . . . *in my mind.* If David Boyd had known that I actually liked him (and to what an extent!) he would've been shocked.

I managed to conceal my love for him entirely. I worshiped him in the private way of a thirteen-year-old girl who'd find romantic exposure almost as mortifying as wearing a two-piece bathing suit to the community swim club. Years later, I learned the downside of emotionally jumping the gun: Men don't like it! It makes them feel pressured and uptight. And peevishly accuse you of being *needy.*

Jumping to romantic conclusions* about a fledgling romance is always dangerous because you run the risk of accidentally improving the story you wrote (either all by yourself, or with the help of excitable girlfriends) while you're out on a third date. It'll make most men want to bolt right out of your door, right after they feel you up.

Scientific Fact: You can't remove the observer from the experiment. When you become too smitten with your subject, you run the risk of losing your keen powers of observation. If you count your chickens before they hatch, you'll also miss important cues screaming, "*Danger! Abort mission!*"

WARNING: Men will initially be on their best behavior to try to convince you that they're the great guys they've smartly deduced you need them to be . . . after all, it's so much easier to get laid that way!

Now to be fair, even the most seasoned Romantic Researcher will be tempted to forget her basic training and act like a total teenager (novice) in the field when being courted by a hot-ass man. She may make silly manhandling mistakes (like confessing how long she's been sex-free) and wind up butt-naked in a Hummer. *So stay alert:* Don't contaminate your romantic research by throwing caution**to the wind.

Solution: Slow down! There are HUGE gaps of intel missing. Trust is created over the course of time, when a man's *actions* also match his *words*. To protect yourself from unnecessary dating disappointment, call up a trusted member of your Mantrap Pack and run your romantic findings by her. Getting a second opinion will ensure that you keep following good manhandling protocol.

It'll also prevent you from getting so looped that you can't see the forest for the trees, and the birds and the bees.

---

* Romantic projection
** Your panties

Romantic Rule: If you're on page 126 of Love Story and he's just swiping through profiles on Tinder, your romance may be Much Ado About Nothing!

Or if he's just a plaything, just break out the Karma Sutra and have fun getting on the same page, together!

Stop Filling in the Blanks

You both love Victorian novels, having sex in broom closets, and eating key lime pies. You think, "*Mon Dieu! This man is perfect for me!*"

Or is he?

WARNING: Faulty romantic research will make excitable women jump to inaccurate conclusions.

Example: Your date arrives right on time, and you ask him to have a seat on the couch while you decide which handbag to use. As you slink back into the living room, you observe him trying to play with your very unfriendly cat . . .

> Dot 1: "Oh, look at kitty," you think to yourself. "He really likes the New Guy! . . . Uh-oh . . . kitty's trying to crawl up New Guy's shirt and sit on his head. OUCH! That must've hurt, but he's not even getting mad. Wow, what a good sport!"

> Dot 2: "I love him!"

> Dot 3: "He's going be an amazing dad!"

Now, I, ask you, how did you get from dot one to dot three? Uh-oh. You connected another dot . . . while we were talking!

> Dot 4: "We'd have gorgeous kids!"

And another . . .

> Dot 5: "He would look so adorable coaching Little League!"

You just connected the dots and drew the picture that you wanted to see! See?

And now you quickly start to color it in. What you don't know is that Howard recently had a vasectomy. When he blurts it out six months from now, you'll let it go right by: "Well, it's reversible! I'm sure he'll get his plumbing fixed once we're engaged!"

Problem: You fail to have this conversation with Howard right now. Oh, you'll have the talk all right, two years from now. And girl, you are gonna be pissed!

In the meantime, you'll want to believe that what you hope to be true, *will* be.

Faulty Romantic Towers.

Commonly referred to as "building castles in the air," Romantic Faulty Towers are constructed through a combination of romantic wish fulfillment and willful denial. Instead of connecting the dots and seeing a skull and crossbones staring back at you, you'll cleverly move the dots around and make a picture that's more to your liking.

"Hey, if I erase dot thirty-two and just move it over here, that skull and crossbones actually looks like . . . a crown! I love crowns!"

We have now reached the end of objectivity and sanity. Your friends shake their heads collectively and say, "What on earth do you see in him? He's a skirt chaser, a gambler, a goofball, a nitwit! We just don't get it!" but you'll be completely incapable of seeing it. You fell in love with the pretty picture you drew and won't take it off the fridge.

Romantic Rule: *When you stop seeing what's happening (denial) and you start making up your own story, you'll usually start to believe it!*

WARNING: Connecting the dots and drawing your own picture will blur your romantic vision. "Wishful Thinking" is a terrible time wasting trap. It'll cause you to fall for men whose goals are completely at odds with yours, and pretend that they'll magically transform *all by themselves* into the men of your dreams someday. Unfortunately, that day is so not right now! This is also called Romance Novel Writing 101.*

When women connect the dots, they cannot correctly (or quickly) assess their suitors. This lack of discernment will cause them to fall for unsuitable characters, and mistakenly reject men of real value.

The upside: Not being able to spot Mr. Wrong soon enough is a terrible waste of a girl's time, but often an excellent use of her lingerie!

If this sounds like you, don't despair. You just need to get a little dating technology under your garter belt. (Or black belt.)

MANDATORY HOMEWORK: If you just started dating a "special someone" last week and think he might be the One, ask yourself the following questions:

---

* Feel free to send your fantasy writing to, support@laurenfrances.com

1. Have you had this feeling before?
2. How many times? (Did I hear you say twelve?)
3. Are you basing your current feelings on intuition, or absolute *certainty?*

If your intuition is accurate 100 percent of the time, call me. I've lost an earring and I can't find it anywhere! For the rest of you who are positive your plane's going to crash (but it doesn't), are sure you'll never fall in love again (and you do), or find tarantulas in the bathtub that turn out to be garden spiders, you need to fact-check your intuition against the red pen of time itself because it'll take months before you figure out exactly who you're swapping spit with.

Q: *Why did God make stilettos?*

A: So a woman would watch her step while being courted, and walk through, and not run past, the courtship phase of her romance!

And that's a fact.

Mistaking Chemistry for Compatibility

Even the most no-nonsense woman can be swept off her feet by intense arousal, confusing physical chemistry with emotional compatibility.

COMPATIBILITY *n* 1. a feeling of sympathetic understanding 2. You both love tofurky and dream of living in a hemp village in Tucson.

Romantic Rule: *Sexual chemistry proves that you're compatible in one room . . . the bedroom!*

You need to get along in the living room, the kitchen, and dining room, too. So let's snap you out of your sex coma and find out where your relationship is really headed. And put your pants back on. They're right over there. Under the sofa. Thank you.

How Compatible Are You?

Every relationship has day-to-day conflicts. These can be smoothed out by tolerance, patience, and mutual loving-kindness. Conflicting agendas and habits, however, turn even the most epic lovers into sparring partners. When partners have different plans for their relationship's destination, it's inevitable that they won't keep happily winging away for any extended period of time. They'll either drift apart, fight for control, or get their needs hijacked by the other. That's why it's imperative to check for compatibility *outside* of the bedroom before hopping onboard.

When partners have different plans for their relationship's destination, it's inevitable that they won't keep happily winging away for any extended period of time. They'll either drift apart, fight for control, or get their needs hijacked by the other. That's why it's imperative to check for compatibility outside of the bedroom before hopping on-board.

Romantic Rule: When partners have different agendas, it's inevitable that their conflicting needs will disrupt their long term happiness.

The Compatibility Coordinates Checklist

Always make sure to interrogate men thoroughly before choosing to give them the gift of your exclusivity. The answers to these questions will reveal whether they're really worth it!

	YES	NO
Do you have the same relationship goals? (Marriage, open relationship, exclusive relationship without marriage?)	＿＿	＿＿
Do you have compatible religious beliefs?	＿＿	＿＿
Do you both want to have children?	＿＿	＿＿
Do you want to live in the same location?	＿＿	＿＿
Do you want the same kind of lifestyle?	＿＿	＿＿

	YES	NO
Do you have similar habits? (Smoking, drinking, vegetarian)	____	____
Do you or your partner have a habit or compulsion or secret that could undermine the well-being and trust of the other person? (Active addiction, penchant for cheating, criminal record)	____	____
Do you have the same values system?	____	____
Do you agree on how to handle your finances — joint or otherwise?	____	____
Do you have deal breakers that would prevent your relationship from culminating in the fulfillment of your relationship goals?	____	____

Romantic Rule: Knowledge is power, so glean important information about your real compatibility with men as soon as possible. Don't mistake a Vulture for a darling Robin Redbreast ever again!

The Velvet Hammer
The Art of Invisible Interrogation

The best way to extract this information is to slip qualifying questions into any conversation. Talking in a casual way won't alarm him, and he'll chime in quite naturally as a matter of course. An overt interrogation is never advisable (unless you're hammering out the terms of your relationship . . . which makes it a conversation, not an interrogation). Always remember to bring up topics that would be deal breakers for you. Cover only one or two of the following questions per "session."

Wondering what his plans are for the future? Try this: "I'd love to live in the hills, and swap my SUV for a Tesla. Where do you see yourself living five years from now?"

Concerned about how he handles the money, honey? Then toss this his way: "I need to hire a financial planner. Do you have someone that you work with? I'd love to hear your experience with that."

If you're curious about if he has a pre-nup on his mind:
"My coworker's fiancé hit her with a pre-nup the day after their engagement party . . . and she makes more than he does! She was shocked. They should've handled that discussion before the wedding invitations went out, don'tcha think?"

Or "I have a friend who called off her engagement because her fiancé just told her he'd refuse to raise their children with religion. And she's a Sunday school teacher! That conversation happened a wee bit late, don't you think?"

You get the idea. Talking about potential deal breakers in an offhanded way will allow you to discover valuable information without directly confronting or startling your birds. Having a light touch is best, and these conversations are a *must.*

Note: Unlike the three-hit rule in Battleship, one strike on this list may be enough to torpedo any romance, so find answers to these questions as soon as you're able. For the record, it's possible to survive major incompatibilities and differences as long as you both don't pretend they'll magically disappear, and you take responsibility for what you're both signing up for. You may successfully survive major incompatibilities if both partners "agree to disagree," and come up with a workable compromise. Relationship negotiation and communication always rules the roost!

MANDATORY HOMEWORK: Get a red pen; make a list of the pros and cons of your relationship. Then make a list of all of the things you are looking for in a man, and see if the two columns match up, Buttercup!

Flush 'Em Out of the Bush!

It takes years for some women to discover that the men they are exclusive with, and completely in love with, had hidden objections about them *right from the beginning*; objections that have prevented them from committing fully!

Q: *Why don't men tell you the truth from the very outset instead of wasting your time?*

The answer is simple. They don't want you to think they're bad guys. They know that breaking the news would only hurt your feelings and decrease their odds of bedding you again, so they totally fail to see the upside.

What men don't realize is that your feelings will ultimately be hurt anyway and so much more so three years down the road! So, to save yourself a lot of time and heartache, use this brilliant manhandling maneuver that a colleague of mine invented to flush unworthy men out of out of the bush.

Case Study: Flush 'Em Out of the Bush! Andrea, 38, TV producer/writer

"I hate being rejected, so I cut to the chase very quickly. In the after-glow, right after we've had fabulous sex for the first or second time, I look over and say, "Dirk, I think you're amazing, but I just don't think things could ever work out between us. I'm so bummed!" Flabbergasted, the guy will always ask me, "Why?!"

Then I list all of the things that I fear he'll ultimately have a problem with:

I live thirty miles away.

I have a pet iguana.

I'm eight years older than you.

I'm a nudist Buddhist flutist.

I just throw down the gauntlet. If he doesn't put up a fight to keep seeing me, or worse, actually agrees with me, I know he's not the One. We've had our fun and now I'm done. It's better to get thrown out of the car going ten miles per hour than sixty!

But if he says, "I love older women! And you can practice your flute in the nude for me anytime. Or on my flute for that matter. Come on baby, I'm crazy about you, I want to keep seeing you," then I know that this man is worth my time. He's reassured me that he's comfortable with things that I could not or *would not* ever want to change about myself, and that he can handle my baggage. He's fought for the right to keep dating me, and to keep petting my iguana!"

Romantic Rule: *It's better to get thrown out of the car going ten miles per hour, than sixty!*

You Can't Turn a Raven Into a Dove

All men, even Pink Flamingos, live by the motto "If it ain't broke, don't fix it.*"

*Translation: "Don't bother trying to change our relationship, or me. Well, on second thought, maybe you can buy me some sexy underpants."

MAN FACT: *All men want to be loved exactly the way they are. They don't want to have to change for us, even if they lie and say they really, really want to. They just said that because they really, really want to have sex with you!*

The list of things he is attached to includes, but is not strictly limited to:

· Every single one of his bad habits

· The leaky beanbag chair in his living room

· His moronic friends

· Flatulence, belching, and knuckle cracking

Negotiables: His clothing, grooming, and, god willing, back waxing. In other words, anything on his person that rubs up against you and totally grosses you out.

Non-negotiables: The big stuff. And also a bunch of the small stuff too.

Hundreds of years of research have shown that no woman, no matter how determined, can change a Raven into a Dove. It just won't work. He'll simply resist, resent, and then reject!

MAN FACT: *Never date a man's potential. It'll only drive you insane. With men, what you see really is what you get.*

Tip: When you move in together, you can throw out his crappy stuff. Just blame it on the movers.

sixteen

Flock Consciousness in the Field

"Oh just look at her, Melly! She's flirting with every man in sight."

"Don't be angry with her, India dear. Scarlett's so attractive all the men just naturally flock to her."

If you've been following this Man Plan, your romantic roster will be teeming with activity. You may find yourself in a new predicament: instead of being date-free, you'll become seriously over-booked! It's time to learn how to create a pecking order so you'll be able to date more than one man at a time without creating a cock-fight.

Putting Men in a Pecking Order

Romantic Rule: Don't let men clip your wings!

It's important to set boundaries with your new feathered friends. There's *no reason* to give new flock members information about the competition. Never reveal facts about your romantic roster until a man cares about you enough to ask about your relationship goals and asks you to enter into a committed relationship with him. If a man asks invasive questions, keep your lip zipped and steer the conversation to neutral topics, like metaphysics or the weather.

Love Script: You're out eating linguine, when all of a sudden your date casually says, "So, are you dating anyone else, Angela?"

Lob back: "Well, I'm dating, but it's nothing serious." This is a line poached from men themselves! And it works. Even if you aren't dating anyone it makes you sound desirable, sets a boundary, and protects your privacy.

Or try this elegant one-liner: "I'm single at the moment." And smile!

Tip: Never let a man press you for more information than he's earned. Until a man's ready to commit, and you are too, all he needs to know is that you like him enough to keep dating him and enjoying your clams.

Romantic Rule: *Your exclusivity is a privilege that a man must earn. Knowledge about your calendar should remain top secret until a real commitment is made.*

The Secret Bargaining Power of Your Exclusivity

Imagine you owned a lovely home on a piece of prime real estate. You watered the lawn, manicured the bushes, painted the interior, and put your house on the market. You'd never sell it at a rock bottom price, fearing that no one else would make an offer. Instead, you'd wait for decent offers from multiple buyers, and only close the deal when you got the proposal that you really wanted, maybe for even *more* than you wanted.

Unless you have severely undervalued your hot property!

REALITY CHECK: The Romantic Researcher always applies the "sellers market theory" to her relationships.

Question: Would you only show your property to a buyer who wasn't sure he really wanted to live there? Even if he said he liked it, even loved it, but wasn't quite ready to buy *(because he secretly thought that he'd find something better).* And while he was *"finding himself"* and *"figuring things out,"* you agreed to refuse to take bids from other buyers. Instead, you put the property on hold for him indefinitely, let him live in it for free, gave away your cats because he was allergic to them . . . and slept with him, too!

If this sounds way too familiar, you've probably fallen for—and into—a terrible time-wasting trap more commonly known as **Serial Monogamy.**

> SERIAL MONOGAMY *v.* You voluntarily commit yourself to a string of relationships that fail to yield long-term commitment, marriage, or family. You (unwisely) agree to open-ended monogamy in the hopes that men will step up if you just love 'em enough.*
> You agreed to take yourself off the market for a man who's not ready to fully commit to you because you're either (a) having amazing sex with him, or (b) he mentioned that he wanted to get married "someday" when you went hiking together.

You hang in there until you realize that you're wasting your time, and then do it all over again, with someone new.

NEWSFLASH: The typical male has no reason to believe that being a "boyfriend" for long stretches of time is actually a problem. And it isn't, *for him.* Men can have children when they're sixty. Who wouldn't want to keep the audition process going as long as possible if they could get away with it?

Men love No-Time-Frame Dating because if you agree to it, they don't have to worry about competing for you with other men. When you give up your exclusivity without clear terms, they get the luxury of taking you out of the field and keeping you in "audition mode" indefinitely. No-Time-Frame Dating allows men to date you, have sex with you, even be monogamous with you, and still never marry you! This is exactly how we let men take minimum risks while receiving maximum pleasure.

---

*This is like offering a man an uncollateralized loan of your emotional capitol!

Romantic Rule: Always prequalify your Lovebirds to see if they have a real emotional investment in your relationship before taking yourself off the market, and get rid of the men who are just browsing.

Healthy relationships are mergers between two partners whose terms should be negotiated up front. In days of yore, marriage was a looked upon as a business contract between two families. Thankfully, our fathers don't have to bribe men with dowries to marry us anymore. Now the men are supposed to commit to us for free (for the love of us.) When women don't speak up, they passively supply what men want, by default.

If you keep winding up on your knees instead of the other way around, you're probably using the outmoded **On a Wing and a Prayer Man Plan.**

ON A WING AND A PRAYER MAN PLAN:
You cross your fingers and just "go with the flow," in the hopes that things will magically work out if you leave things up to chance (aka your boyfriend).

REALITY CHECK: When you refuse to speak up, it'll only be the luck of the draw if you find a man who's emotionally mature enough, reckless enough, or psychic enough to provide exactly you what you want. That's why it's so important to know what your dating requirements are, and communicate them in language a man can understand.

Mantra: Negotiations begin today!

Romantic Researchers, Remember!

• It's not who you've been dating but *how* you've been dating, that's usually the source of a romantic problem.

• Dating isn't a mini-relationship, it's a pleasurable fact-finding mission.

• Dating will naturally result in *The Survival of the Fittest* when you wisely follow the laws of natural selection.

• Flock Consciousness is the antidote to the endless dating trap!

A Bird in the Hand
Is Worth Two in the Bush!

If you're wise, you'll never bring up the topic of exclusivity with a man ever again. You'll wait for *him* to bring it up with you, instead.

Romantic Rule: *Always let men press you for exclusivity, and not the other way around.*

When men fall in love, they'll pressure you for a commitment of monogamy all by themselves, usually right *after* they start having sex with you. They'll want to make sure that you'll refuse sexual invitations from other available males. For men, getting you to agree to monogamy can be translated thusly: *"I won't cheat, if you don't!"* or *"I'd like to put you on hold and figure out how I feel about you somewhere down the road."*

Agreeing to this sloppy arrangement is exactly how many women lose years of their lives to Mr. Wrong, who seemed so very right at the outset! When women fail to specify how much time they'll be willing to invest in an exclusive relationship before seeing their long-term goals accomplished, they often wind up spinning their wheels with inappropriate men. Or allow relationships with Lovebirds capable of pair-bonding to drift.

Note: If you're very young or just up for some fun, you may choose to wing it,* too. But if you're ready to roost, please pay close attention to this:

Romantic Rule: *Once a man asks you for your exclusivity, it's your cue to quickly negotiate the terms of your surrender!*

THE PECKING ORDER PRINCIPLE:

A woman should never surrender her exclusivity until a man offers a relationship whose terms and conditions are truly acceptable. Resist the temptation to give up your exclusivity until someone has given you a very good reason to do so.

---

* Commit to an exclusive, monogamous No-Time-Frame-Dating kind of relationship.

Step One: Separate the Men from the Boys

When a man asks you for exclusivity, you'll need to:

1. Make sure he has compatible relationship goals
2. Set a time limit with about how long you'll be willing to "test drive" your relationship.
3. Be willing to have direct and timely conversations with your partner and find out what his Man Plan is for his "relationship future."

Note: All men have one, they just don't like to blurt them out. Especially if they don't view you as "the One" they'd like to commit to, somewhere on down the road.

4. Be brave! (And be honest with yourself). If he doesn't want the kind of relationship you're seeking, (or want to have it with you!), then he needs to be dropped from your flock, Sister. Let's find you a better Mister!

The Good News: If he's the right man for you, this "talk" won't scare him away, but bring him closer to you. He'll hop closer, be happy to open up and share his happy thoughts.

Words to Live by: *Don't squander time. It's the stuff life is made of!*

Step Two: Throw Salt on His Tail

Love Script: Once a man asks you for exclusivity, you need to find out what his plans are for himself *before* you agree to "go steady" with him, and not after!

Here's how to find out what's in his noggin: Start by communicating your personal relationship goals to him in a simple sentence or two: "I'd love to see more of you, Humphrey. But you should know that I'm looking for (*Examples: marriage, family, an open relationship, etc.)* And what about you?"

If he chirps back in agreement that his goals are compatible with yours, however, bravo! Take this lovebird at his word. Now you'll need to clearly state what the expiration date on your "exclusive offer" is.

Love Script: Say, "I'm thrilled that you'd like to move things forward with me, Hank. It's great that you have the same relationship goals. Are you ready for *(whatever he said he wanted)* at this point in your life, or is that something you'd like to create down the road?"

And now LISTEN UP. He is going to share his MAN PLAN.

WARNING: If this sentence rubbed him the wrong way or seems to come as something of shock, you can choose to drop him, or keep him incubating in your flock. Beware the Lame Duck who flaps around and doesn't meet your conversation halfway. If you spot him in your midst, have a little fun with him like this: *"I hope you want a big family, Jack, because I sure do. Twins run in my family!"*

   Gulp!

WARNING: Upon hearing this statement uttered by you, emotionally unavailable men will (predictably) start squawking about how they don't want to feel *"pressured"* into *(engagement, marriage, pregnancy)* and start singing the *Battle Hymn of the (Male) Republic:* "What? Wait a minute! How can you expect me to know after only one month of dating you if or when I'll feel like (proposing, getting pregnant, buying a home)? I hate being pressured! My last girlfriend tried to try to pressure me and I broke up with her."

   If he starts trilling this predictable little tune, don't go into a tailspin. Simply defy his flighty logic with a little dose of reality: *"I understand you don't want to feel pressured, Rich. But what about me? My time frame needs to be considered too, and I just want to make sure I'm compatible with you."*

And then zip you're lip!

Tip: Whoever speaks next loses ground, (I hate to say *loses,* but this is a negotiation, so stating your question and then waiting for an answer will be a very effective way to suss him out, and hold your power.)

   Lay your cards on the table, and don't flinch. See what he comes up with, because he just might surprise you!

If he says, "*Well, I'd love to get married someday*" (or states goals that are in alignment with yours), then say, "Great! I'd be happy to give this a whirl for (?) number of months, to see how we click. *(He deserves this because he was cagey about having simple relationship time-table talk.)* You're underlining that you heard his ambivalence, and aren't cornering him into something he isn't really committing to!

This logic is very hard, dare I say *near impossible*, for a man to refute. You've told him that while you respect his time frame, he'll need to respect *yours* too. So zip your lip and observe him. He's either going to fly straight into the windowpane, or do laps in big slow circles and come up with a snappy comeback.

"*Hey, I've been faithful to you since the day we met, but if there's someone else you'd rather date, I won't stand in your way!*" He might even throw in a cocky "*I'm not worried about the competition anyway.*"

Or if he's passive aggressive - or a lawyer - he might try to manipulate you like this: "*I think that the best kind of relationship is when two people are monogamous because they want to be, not because they need to be, or a piece of paper says that they have to be!*"

If you hear this adolescent tune, quickly take the air out of his sails this way: "*Are you really all right with me dating other people, Dick? If that's the case, it's okay, but you should know it'll change the way that I continue to date you.*" At this point, your bird will probably start turning green and ask in a tight little voice what in God's name you mean.

MAN FACT: *All men are like Icarus. They don't know they're flying too close to the sun until you bring them back down to earth.*

So call his blustery bluff thusly: "*Well, darn. I'd probably feel okay seeing you once a week, but I wouldn't want to chat every day, because it sounds like you don't want to get too attached. I'm not quite sure how I'd feel about sleeping together. It might be okay, but I'm not sure how that'll make me feel. Let's play it by ear.*"

Do not utter one more word! You've seen him, raised him, called him (and cornered him!) into showing you his hand. Men who have real partnership potential will now fold, back down, knock it off, grow up, and ante up. (Set a time frame that's fair for the both of you.) *C'est magnifique!* You've taught him a wonderful trick called **Stepping on Command**.

Note: Write this date in your calendar. Then follow the instructions on page 210 one month prior to it.

If you find, however, that your suitor starts to balk, behaves like a Bat out of Hell, or resists this talk, don't become alarmed. He may need a little space to contemplate his (bleak) future without you. Don't cave in! Hold your ground. Men who aren't sociopaths (aka unrepentant womanizers), will often have a complete change of heart within several days a month, or even two months. If you wait him out he may have a *total turnabout*. But he doesn't, please don't fret or pout! Don't despair! Don't eat inexpensive chocolates, or start tearing out your hair.

Romantic Rule: *Selfish and immature men run from emotional accountability as fast as they can.*

Let Peter Pan fly out the window, and go find yourself a man!

You Should Only Surrender
Your Exclusivity to a Man When...

1. You've thoroughly qualified your Lovebird.

2. He says he shares the same relationship goals that you do, and is committed to realizing them *with you.*

3. You both have a time-frame in which to accomplish them. Then you can date him exclusively with your conscience clear.

Nice job on the fancy footwork, my dear!

The Birds and the Bees

We're not above birds; let's misbehave!
-Cole Porter

Women bait and men desperately try to catch. It's genetic. When a woman understands that men really do love the hunt, she isn't actually cockteasing but agreeably encouraging a predatory chase. That's why it's always a good idea to prolong the make-out phase of your relationship before flinging open Pandora's box. Here's to the noble art of keeping your eyes open and your thong on!

Pecking Order
(aka the Artful Dodger)

Mysterious, barbaric, and arcane—what more needs to be said about the art of female seduction? What more . . . other than it's also beautiful. And that, like other pastimes involving the pursuit of game for pleasure, it's rich with contradictions.

Q: What's the average number of dates you go on before going all the way?

One Date?   Two date?   Three dates?   More

According to the Nobel laureates at Cosmo, 76 percent of the respondents answered three dates. Bluntly put, men and women both seem to agree that it's three strikes, they're out, or three? dates, he's in! Unfortunately, this courtship schedule is far too brief for most women to conduct anything resembling proper "research." Unless your male is going to be just a plaything, the wise man handler always benefits by artfully cockteasing a man first before diving completely undercover.

Romantic Rule: Don't have casual sex with a man whom you're falling for until he's falling in love with you, too.

Pheromones and Oxytocin:
The Twin Chemistry Set Called Love

Sex doesn't make men fall in love with you. Love makes men fall in love with you. But sex helps!

—Lauren Frances

Irritating Fact: Mother Nature wisely predicted that women would never tolerate the bad habits of most men, so she decided to drug us to ensure the propagation of the species. She gave us a "cuddle hormone" called oxytocin that bonds us instantly to any man with whom we have even passable sex. And once they make us orgasm, our goose is cooked no matter how much we may have despised them before they got our thong off. Then, the more sex you have with this fiend, the more bonded you'll become, until just seeing him, smelling him, or finding his crumpled shirt in your laundry basket will chemically activate you with rapturous feelings of love and make you want to put up with him long enough to impregnate you (seems to be Mother Nature's reasoning here).

Much More Irritating Fact: Men possess this hormone, too, but in such ridiculously small amounts that it isn't enough to produce the desire for monogamy.*

Mother nature was afraid that women, drugged or not, would find men too smelly and irritating to keep indoors, so she came up with a little backup plan. She gave men a *completely different* primal genetic directive: "*Go forth, young harem master, and get your freak on. Cast your seed upon the man, and avoid capture!*"

This explains why it takes men so much more time to emotionally connect to women (from their dick to the brain and then to the heart), and also explains why they violently resist *enemy capture (monogamy)*. They're actually fighting against Mother Nature herself!

Romantic Rule: *Men like to think of their bodies as a temple, with a lot of worshippers.*

Men will try to get into your panties first and conduct important relationship research second. And if they do emotionally step up after sex, always pay very close attention because, unlike you (the love drugged), they're falling for you stone-cold sober!

---

* Sadly, I did not make this up!

Once men swoop you up in their big sexy talons, they'll try to get as physically close to you as two separate people can who aren't Siamese twins. He may also, however, fly right out the window after he finishes ravishing you (the come-and-go migratory pattern).

Birds of prey fall in love over time by actively pursuing you, thinking about you when you're apart, and then having sex with you (aka hunting). By artfully cockteasing a man, you do him such a favor... you give him the space he needs to have a feeling reach two feet higher than his belt buckle!

Man Fact: *Getting him hard won't make his heart* soft, *but falling in love with you over time will.*

The cocktease takes one step forward and two tiny steps back to inflame a man's desire. The rogue will make a valiant attempt to seduce her, but denied an easy victory, he redoubles his efforts. Although a man may get into a pet at being denied his quick pleasure, he'll love nothing more than this sweet torment. His manhood will be completely at the ready! So after he makes proper oaths of fealty, allow him his spoils . . . and let him rip the bodice from your heaving bosom.

—The Confessions of Dr. L

Slowing men down gives them a wonderful opportunity to realize that you're more than just a snack. Don't let him devour you right away. Make him do it for *hours and hours* over the course of several weeks at least! Rediscover the kiss, and I promise you this: When you make out in restaurants, bars, and the front seats of cars, or up against the wall in the hall . . . *he'll want to rip your panties off with his teeth.*

Romantic Rule: Don't go into a sex coma until you've thoroughly fact-checked your man, administered verbal truth serum, and quizzed him like a pro.

MANHANDLING MANEUVER: Perform these interrogations while wearing black leather boots and gloves, and if he passes your test, keep 'em on when everything else comes off.

How to Keep Your Man on Simmer

When you need to slow a man down, here's a useful tip: Don't invite him in, until you're ready to invite him *all* the way in!

MAN FACT: *Once you let men indoors, they just wanna get naked!*

Here are two basic facts about the breeding habits of the typical sexually stimulated male:

1. Men will have sex anywhere, be it a tool shed, a pool shed, or aisles S through V at your local library. Your first several dates should be in public places, and end on your doorstep. Once you bring men indoors, they're liable to raise the roof by crowing like Rowdy Roosters before sunrise. (*See* Woodpecker.)

2. Giving a man "sex to remember you by" doesn't make him want you more, but thinking about ravishing you upon his return certainly will!

Male Breeding Manners and the Two-for-One Rule

Men need to learn how to wait their turn, especially since their turn requires so little encouragement, once it finally comes up. This is the real logic behind the seemingly arcane practices of chivalry that are alive and well today. Helping you on with your coat, opening your car door, and walking behind you while exiting a restaurant. Mastering chivalrous good manners are a kind of "sex prep" for young males brilliantly designed to train men to come second, *and not first*, in the bedroom.

Romantic Rule: Men shouldn't think about satisfying themselves till they've made their girlfriends see godhead (orgasm) at least once.*

Twice is definitely better and is the gentleman's rule of thumb. Besides, as any good lover knows, once you get a girl going, she'll go all night. Never feel bad if your man is slaving away. Hard work is good for them . . . and besides, if you make them do their duty, *maybe they'll get better at it.*

To quote Mike Dugan: *"Women don't take longer . . . women last longer!"*

Always insist on the Two-for-One Rule!

Tommy, Can You Feel Me?

Here are two common hand signals that you'll need a heads-up about, (before you start to go down).

Does this sound familiar? You're making out with a man, when all of a sudden he reaches over, grabs your hand, and just puts it on his dick (which is now the size of a baseball bat). Even if you were deaf, dumb, and blind, it would be impossible to miss.

Most women have been on the receiving end of this gesture, but some of you may be confused as to its meaning. Allow me to clarify it for you, and yes, you may borrow my pen.

This is the international mating signal in every language for *"Our make out is now over. We are going to the next level. I hope I brought a condom!"*

It's just like baking. Once the yeast has risen, it's biscuits, baby. He'll want to show you the size of his rolling pin.

---

* Don't fake!

WARNING: Men who are well endowed often do this as a pre-view of what's to come. *Literally.* Unless you are really ready to go all the way, right now, you had best remove your hand immediately and back away from it. He has now switched into "Need-to-Breed mode," and you're asking for trouble if you try to make him "behave," regain his composure, and go back in time to the 1950s. Once your hand is on his dick, he'll think there is absolutely no reason to turn back the hands of time and just "make out" again!

MAN FACT: *Men like to move forward and not backward, in wartime campaigns and in the sack.*

Decent men want you to feel comfortable. They don't stop dating women who set reasonable limits. They don't really expect you to give them exactly what they want, when they want it. Good guys invest the time that it takes for the both of you to get on the same page when they're really interested in you.

Men *will* get mad if you purposely confuse them (saying yes and then no and then yes and then no), or unfairly insisting that they sexually reset their c(l)ock to pre-make-out position.

Translation: Bitch.

Soothing the Savage Bird

Follow these five easy steps to soothe the savage beast:

1. Simply remove your hand and say, **"Whoa, I am sooo thirsty, I'll be back in a jiffy."**
2. Exit the room and give him a minute to regain his composure.

3. Return and say: *"Mmmmnn . . . here's some nice cold water."*

4. If he tries to pick up right where he left off, say, **"I'm so flattered, but I'm not quite ready to go there yet. Can we slow down a little? I need to catch my breath!"** And fan yourself with your hand, as a visual.

5. Don't sit down again! He'll get the message. Simply open the door, have a good-night peck, and say, **"I can't wait to see you again, Marco!"** and then shoo him right out of the door.

Romantic Rule: *Respect the dick. Immediately back away from it and don't continue to handle it, if you're not ready to rock it!*

Got it?

Note: While there are more than six thousand languages in the world, all men still use "primal sexual sign language."

Proof: Evolution is a mere blip in the mind of God.

The Handyman
& How to keep him at Bay

The next hand signal that unruly men often employ is wonderfully illustrated in this field study conducted by a colleague, Katarina. Katarina is a curvaceous brunette and full of fun. Here's how she wrangled a randy handyman . . . it's ingenious.

Action & Adventure: A Case Study:

"I once dated an action-adventure film director whom we'll call 'the Handyman.' Even though he had a terrible reputation for screaming on the set and womanizing, he seemed nice enough at first. I was newly single and thought, 'Oh, what the hell?' I was up for some fun.

We went out and everything seemed perfect, until I noticed, to my dismay, that while we were making out, he had his hand in his *pants*. On a first date, I found this to be outrageous behavior. He wanted action all right, and I was unable to say, *"Cut!"*

"When he didn't stop, I couldn't help but feel insulted. I mean, what was I, chopped liver? He said he was *"too turned-on" to stop*. Well, okay, I thought. Good excuse. The next time we went out , (yeah I know, I'm an idiot), I wore a scarf just in case. And when the Handyman started to reach for his gun, I was ready. I looked him in the eye and said, *"Hold out your hands, Mister!"* and then whipped the scarf from my neck and tied his hands quickly together. I then proceeded to kiss him.

"This drove him wild, and it was really fun until he started begging me to untie him. To my dismay his hand went right back to his remote. He was madly in love with it and refused to keep his hands off it. When I finally said, *"Hey, bud! What about me? I'm feeling a little left out over here,"* he snapped, *"It's not tit for tat! I'll take care of you next time."*

Next time? *As if!*

eighteen

Sex and the Single Bird

Letting men into the henhouse!

You must always guard your eggs like a farmer in the dell. The very best way to protect yourself is to be exclusive, go to the same doctor, and then get tested for everything under the sun, *together*. But if you're in the first flush and in more of a rush, the easiest way to discuss barnyard complaints is as simple as this: Before you're in any danger of contracting something, say, "Do you have anything I'm not going to want to catch?"

Hear him out. And then it's your turn. If you're both magically STD free, you still have to use a condom until you're sexually exclusive with each other. It's always chivalrous if the man comes prepared to "cloak his dagger." But if he isn't prepared, you should be. Always BYOB (Bring Your Own Birth Control) and then remember to *use it*!

Romantic Rule: *Men will try to escape wearing a condom about as fast as a cat getting out of a collar.*

Use the following love scripts to exert Vulcan (vaginal) mind control over men when they're attempting to avoid plastic capture:

If he tries:"I'm not that kind of guy. I don't just carry them around in my wallet."
Quip back: "Well, I must be that kind of girl because I've got one in my purse!"

"I forgot to bring them."
"Well, there's a 7-Eleven right down the street. And grab me a Diet Coke while you're at it."

"I can't feel anything! I want to take it off!"
"No problem. Let's watch a rom-com!

"Please, baby, you're so hot, I just can't stop!"
"Okay, down boy! Sit! Stay. Now put this condom on or I'm putting my panties on, Ron."

"I can't get hard wearing one."
"No problem. Let's take some Viagra together. It's amazing."

"I always use one, so I'm safe."
"Wow. What a relief. But if you want to have sex with me, you still need to put on a slipcover.

"Just once, baby, please?"
"Nope. If you want some love, put on a sex mitten, Tom."

"I won't come, I promise I won't come!"
"Aren't you thoughtful! But even if you don't come, you still need to wear a raincoat."

"I'm totally safe; I was tested two months ago."
"I'm glad you're keeping tabs on things. But we need to use protection if you want to get near me with your erection!"

WARNING: Only guys most likely to have STDs use lines like the following:

"Why? I don't have any STD's!"
"Boy, am I relieved! Let's slip on this penis protec-tor. It looks just about your size."

"I never use one!"
"Wow. Let's be friends."

"I won't have sex with you then."
"Finally we agree on something. Ciao!"

nineteen

Male Breeding Displays

Now let's review the sexual displays of the modern breeding male, and some manhandling tips that you won't want to miss!

Early Birds

Some men—sexual narcissists, selfish Lame Ducks, and most eighteen–year-olds—have a nasty habit of being Early Birds. Many Early Birds mistakenly think that just because they're climaxing, *you are too*, and now everybody's happy. Unfortunately, the Early Bird will go right on thinking that you're satisfied unless you correctly train him to put *your* orgasm before his own, which, as we have discussed, is exactly where it should be. This is the real reason why Mother Nature blessed strapping young men and forty-year-old women with identical sex drives . . . so he'd receive the instruction that he so desperately needs from a woman he'll actually *listen* to.

Romantic Rule: Never pretend to be having a ball when to you aren't.

A laissez-faire attitude about your own orgasm is passive negative reinforcement. It lulls men into thinking that their inadequate mating habits are actually satisfying, trains them to be lazy and selfish in the sack, and leaves the problem for the next gal to deal with. Come on, people!

How to Slow Down Your Early Bird

The next time he's racing you to the finish line, slow him down by whispering, "Baby, make me wait," softly in his ear, and then repeat this instruction several times, if necessary. Always look at him with meaning and smile seductively as you say it. You'll be able to tell when the light goes on because his rhythm will automatically slow down and he'll look at you like the first caveman kindling a fire. *Et voilà!* Now we're getting somewhere.

Give him a wicked little grin as a reward, and encourage him to stay the course and slow his pace by repeatedly telling him how good it feels, how big he is, how hot he's making you, blah, blah, blah... you know the drill. Men need repeated verbal encouragement while being sexually retrained, so always praise your bird when he's trying very hard to please you.

If that didn't make an impression, shout, "Darling, the train is moving but I'm not on board! Slow down! You've got to make my whistle blow before you leave the station." This will be so confusing he'll come to a complete halt and stop right in his tracks, I promise you that.

Romantic Rule: Remember, nice guys finish last.

Dominant Crowing Cocks

This rowdy rooster has quite a lot to crow about. He's the master of the multiple orgasm. You may accidentally hyperventilate from excitement, so put the paramedics on speed dial . . . just in case of emergencies.

Because they are sex geniuses, Crowing Cocks can usually mate with females as often as they like and still hope to spread their genes far and wide. Hopefully, for your sake, your Cock will be of the rare monogamous variety, but any man this good in the sack probably got this way because he's had so much practice boning up.

Typically, a Crowing Cock displays his sexual supremacy by quickly putting his chick into a "sex coma." This is usually done in an attempt at relationship intervention. He's hoping you'll be so impressed by his outstanding sexual performance that you'll jump on his erect manhood, go right into a sex coma, and completely forget to have a boundary with him. And he'll usually be right. It will be damned near impossible to imagine how you ever lived without him by the time he's done with you, and he knows it.

If you have a Crowing Cock in your flock, congrats! He's a wonderful addition and can be enjoyed like any fun, forbidden food. Don't forget that this man is, more often than not, just a treat and shouldn't take the place of dinner. But if, in the course of your research, you discover that he's prime for the plucking, too, you'll have hit the jackpot! Who'll be the one crowing then? Why, I think it'll be *you.*

The Master Cock:
Predatory Sex Addicts

Polygamous despots of ancient times have a lot in common with Master Cocks. These adulterous males act like they're single even when they're married. Farmers (and girlfriends have always known that over time), Master Cocks grow less interested in mating repeatedly with the same hen. But when a new female is introduced, our Cock wants to copulate, and he allocates considerably more sperm to his new mate.

WARNING: This heartthrob is impossible to pin down unless you physically *tie* him down (he'll probably suggest you use handcuffs). He's also erratic and dangerous, but this may only add to his allure. Your love affair will feel like you're watching a traffic accident happen in slow motion, but you won't try to put on the brakes because he's so ridiculously hot.

The only way to date a Master Cock is to treat him exactly the way that he treats you: like an illicit tryst at an expensive hotel, or motel, depending on his budget.

Once you're hooked (bedded), he won't have time to see you. He's the master of avoidance and will quickly put you into romantic rotation. He's on tour, on the set, in the studio, or on vacation with the wife. And hunting for more groupies to feed his predatory appetite.

The only way to get over him is to go cold turkey and find a Dodo Bird or immediately buy a vibrator (or both) to expedite your emotional healing.

To lure him, wear a belly shirt and head toward the back of the barn. He'll be surrounded by a gaggle of very hot chicks. Cock-a-doodle-doo, baby!

The Dead Duck

The Dead Duck has a disturbing condition known as "equipment failure." If his little soldier won't stand at attention right away, don't panic. The most experienced researchers often ignore poor posture altogether if it occurs during a first or second engagement in the field. Sometimes the "little general" needs a few skirmishes before taking the hill, so I always advise allowing men a few trial runs before calling in the cavalry.

To resurrect a dead duck: Put him at ease by complimenting his lovely touch and his gorgeous brown eyes, which sear right into the depths of your very soul. Don't comment on his package being MIA, and give him two more chances, if you like him. He probably suffered temporary performance anxiety because you were so damned hot, and he'll soon get over the bump and hump you soon enough.

If he disappoints you three times, however, you're dealing with a psycho/medical problem, and he should be thoughtful enough to stop annoying you and go get the magic from a bottle . . . (Viagra). In this day and age there is absolutely no excuse for a man to be this inconsiderate. It'd be like a woman refusing to wax her undercarriage before date night. But, oh, a slumping soldier is so much worse!

Romantic Rule: *When playing with balls its one, two, three strikes, he's out!*

Now, some will say that all a man needs to be a great lay are two fingers and some determination. *Fact:* The only people who ever say this are men! Every gal wants a raging hard on. After all . . .

Even Mother Nature Believes in Survival of the Stiffest!

Note: A Dead Duck can also be a symptom of a heart condition, so ask him if he's gone to the doc! You might save his life, and wind up being his wife. But if HAS checked it out and it's all ship shape, then he's got "issues."

It's also common that *may refuse* to take V to handle his package, and act like it's an affront to his manhood. He may sulk, or even try to pretend that it's *your* fault he can't perform. We scoff at this! He's definitely the problem, not you, and *everyone* knows it.

PC Rebuttal: Some would say that if a woman doesn't want to be judged by the size of her thighs, she has no right to judge a man who's having trouble maintaining a hard-on. If you're feeling guilty, ponder this . . . *you can still have sex with him no matter what size your ass is.*

MANHANDLING MANEUVER: The best technique for handling a Dead Duck is to offer to take Viagra *with him*. Now, before you get your nose out of joint, consider this: It's no different than walking a youngster to the school bus and helping him get on-board. Viagra is known to have sexually stimulating properties for the ladies, too, and will often result in some earth-shattering orgasms!

Ask your physician for some Viagra samples (don't be nervous, they'll make sympathetic clucking noises), and the next time you and your Dead Duck are together, lean in and suggest with a conspiratorial grin that you both take some V. He'll think it's kinky. Then you can have a little revival meeting lying down. He can thank Jesus, and you can praise the Lord!

Note: Find out if he has a heart condition before he takes it unless you're already in the will.

The Lucky Duck

The Lucky Duck is *any* guy lucky enough to bed you, hon!

Seductive Crooning and Cooing

When men are aroused, they will say almost anything. That is why they are verbally armed and potentially dangerous. They've been dragged to enough chick flicks and have seen enough DeBeers commercials to know exactly which utterances will make you want to trust them with your nakedness.

Seductive Cooing

- "I've always had a crush on you but I thought you'd never go out with me."

- "I feel so comfortable with you it's scary."

- "You remind me of the only woman I've ever loved."

- "I've never been able to talk to anybody the way I can talk to you."

- "I want you to meet my mother."

- "You'd look gorgeous pregnant."

MAN FACT: Men know exactly what women want to hear. This is where the old adage "If his lips are moving, he's lying" comes from.

Also ignore declarations made during sex, like "Let's get married." "I love you." "Let's go to the Bahamas."

The things that a man blurts out during sex are like the deranged rantings of drunkards. He'll usually plead temporary insanity or deny any knowledge of his agitated warbling when he finally comes . . . to.

Romantic Rule: *If your lover makes the same declarations in the light of day, he actually meant them!*

How to Lure a Dodo

If Mr. Right has become your Nemesis Bird, Mr. Right now can be such a boon! Here are some tips to lure a Dodo, and let him know you're in the mood.

FOOLING AROUND *v* 1. having sex with someone who's gorgeous but just too dumb to love. 2. the perfect "go-to" man-management package preferred by the newly single woman just released back into the field, or the too-busy-to-give-a-hoot working woman, or any gal who's just up for fun.

Love Script to Lure the Dodo

Say with enthusiasm: *"I'm not looking for anything serious right now. I hope you don't mind. I'm just up for some fun."* This statement sends a clear message that you're emotionally unavailable and up for a romp. *"Have you ever had sex in a Ferrari?"* will always work too!

Beware: Using these come-hither lines will inspire such enthusiasm, you may wind up with a mandicap.

MANDICAP 1. sex-related injury. 2. usage: As in, "He rode me so hard he gave me a mandicap! I need a bag of frozen peas and a nice long nap."

Clipping His Wings:
Naughty Things Men Try to Get away With and What You Can Do About It

Men nowadays request the most wildly debauched behavior from women whom they barely know with a totally straight face. These men are winging it and trying to see how much they can get away with, so never feel pressured to say yes (unless you really, really want to!). Use the following tips to deflect unwelcome sexual advances from the devilishly deviant Bird . . .

The Boyfriend Exchange Program
(aka Swinging or Partner Swapping)

This occurs when your boyfriend wants to have sex with your best friend and doesn't want to cheat or do the hard work of convincing her himself. He wants you to do it *for* him.

Upside: The Boyfriend Exchange Program is like getting to wear a sweater without taking off the tags for easy returns!

Q: Is it better to swap partners with someone you know or someone you don't know?

A: Unless you do a lot of catalog shopping, I'd definitely recommend knowing the person first. You probably know what looks good on you, and who'd look good *on* you, so I recommend that you take charge of the casting.

To Deflect: If your man asks if you'd ever consider having a ménage à trois with your gal pal, say: *"When Betsey remembers to return my Jell-O mold, I'll consider it. But until then, I'm not lending her my boyfriend!"*

Three Answers for Three-ways: *

HIM: Have you had a threesome before?
YOU: 1. Does the cat count?
   2. I had to give it up. Someone always feels left out and it's never me!
   3. Oh darling, I'm sure you'll do just fine. You're not only funny, you're thoughtful, too!

Romantic Rule: *Always remember that good etiquette dictates that if you swap up, remember to swap back or you'll go from being a swapper to a swiper . . . and that's bad manners!*

The D.I.Y. Porn Dynasty

This is the audiovisual version of the old notch on the belt (and the makings of future blackmail). Guys who want to photograph you for posterity usually wind up showing your posterior to their friends over a beer. These photos and videos can (and often will), be used against you. If you start your own do-it-at-home porn dynasty, always make sure you keep all of the evidence on YOUR phone, and not his. And you can always delete them right after you watch them together! (Do not send them to the cloud!)

To *Deflect:* Say, "We can make one on our honeymoon." Remember to make him sign a waiver, If he's got anything compromising, just get him drunk, and get the password to his cellphone! Photos and videos can haunt you, forever.

Dressing Up and Role-Playing

I think everyone should get spanked by Santa at least *once* in a lifetime.

SPANKER *n* 1. one who spanks.

---

* This course ist often given in France and on American college campuses. (See "Unexplained Lesbianism and the Jell-O Shot."

To Deflect: (Hmm . . . I can't think of one good reason not to try this on for size. Ummm. Wow. I'm stumped. Work on this later.)

Tip: If you're on your knees begging for mercy, remember to wear stilettos!

Knocking On Your Backdoor

This request is a fave of the Bat Out of Hell and the Dirty Bird.

Request: "Baby, can we do it from behind?"

Rebuttal: "Darling, I think a girl's got to save something for the honeymoon, don't you?"

Tip: If a man asks you to engage in this practice, it's always nice to pretend it's your first time!

twenty

Flight Patterns

"Ah, madam," said Lancelot sadly, "I love you only
and no other woman in all the world. But for many
reasons I strive to flee your presence."
—Arthurian Legend

The "flight" response is at the root of a man's need for emotional "space." Depending on the man, his flight patterns may look like short jaunts or long-term adventures.

After several months of gathering data, a pattern should emerge and you'll be able to predict your bird's migration routes and favorite escape pathways.

The Evolution of the Escapee Boyfriend

Modern men are walking around with the same hormonal responses to imminent danger as cavemen. When men perceive a threat to their freedom, their bodies prepare to fight to the death or take flight to escape certain defeat by a superior adversary, *you*. This primal fight-or-flight instinct usually causes an alarmed man to turn tail and flee. So don't blame yourself; it's genetic!

He Flew the Coop

You've been dating intensely for a while and every time you look over your shoulder, he's always right . . . *what?* Wait a minute, where did he go? Uh-oh, sound familiar?

You've just experienced the most frustrating (and mysterious) of all male dating phenoms. You were both on cloud nine but now he needs some "space."

SPACE *n* 1. spaced, or spacing you out. 2. the universe beyond the earth's atmosphere. 3. common male need after prolonged intimacy with a woman. Usage: "I need some space."

You're confused. You thought everything was perfect. So what happened?

Ongoing intimacy with women often triggers the male self preservation directive: Fly low, drop cargo! Your proximity has inadvertently triggered his primal need to fly toward freedom. He longs to soar over the tundra, survey the glorious world unencumbered by emotional baggage (you), and feel the rush of air under his wings. And to look for tiny mice.

Don't worry. After he reassures himself that he's still capable of flight, he'll grow tired of flapping around and land on your doorstep once again, if he loves you. Or if he was really, really into having sex with you. When he returns, the wise man handler won't take his need for space personally. She'll calmly say, "Hi hon."

Translation: I left the cleaver in the kitchen.

The Wild Goose Chase

All men have an inner GPS (Girl Positioning System), which allows them to locate and migrate toward or away from their targeted prey. They also use it to spot and flee from dangerous predators, irritating girlfriends, or angry exes.

Most men are masters at resisting "emotional arrest." When things get too heavy, they try to fly away, just to see if they still can.

Romantic Rule: Don't ever bar the door and prevent a man who's trying to flee your presence from taking flight.

This will only backfire on you. Screaming, crying, vase throwing, and threatening suicide, homicide, or patricide are misguided attempts at manhandling, and you'll pay a huge price for any victory you *think* you've won. Men abhor women who don't respect their right to leave an apartment, conversation, or relationship if they so choose. When men start singing "Freebird," just open the door and let 'em fly away. You can always lock it after them!

If you make a scene every time your man needs space, he'll feel smothered and controlled and look for *even more ways* to flee the relationship. You'll teach him to mistrust you and cause him to become agitated, angry, or passive-aggressive. He may even become sneaky and plotting or downright hostile. Let him go.

Once he does a couple of laps, he'll satisfy his urge and return to you refreshed, attentive, *and human.* So retract your claws and purr.

Short-Looped Migration Pattern
(aka Why Did the Chicken Cross the Road?)

Sometimes men will fly the coop to reassure themselves that they haven't become totally pussy–whipped . . . I mean, domesticated. This is known as a short-looped migration or, in lay terms, poker night.

He majestically surveys the terrain, has a beer, and then flies home. There was nothing in particular that he wanted anyway; he simply needed to get some air, stretch his legs, and prove to himself that the cage door was still open. Sometimes this short jaunt takes only twenty minutes. He'll make a quick run to the store, take the dog for a walk, or make a quick trip to the local watering hole and come right back home. Unless he's drinking Wild Turkey.

Winged Migration
(aka Eccentric Migrations)

The typical American bachelor party is a perfect example of an "eccentric migration." Birds may travel considerable distances from their usual nesting areas (your place) to predictable partying destinations (Vegas!) where they spend several flightless days in drunken revelry.

These debauched migrations lead them pell-mell into the breeding ranges of some scandalously under dressed females. Don't worry, strippers don't want him, they want a tip! So leave them alone and they'll come home, dragging their tail feathers behind 'em.

The Come-and-Go Migration

You threw caution to the winds because you couldn't imagine ever taking him seriously, so you thought, "Screw it," or because he was so damned hot you didn't want to resist. And now you're looking at the telephone and wondering when he'll call.

MAN FACT: *A guy who's flying at warp speed five knows that this is much too fast. He's walking a fine line between hot fun and bad manners. Although this can be delightful in the moment, so is eating an entire box of chocolates.*

STRANGE BUT TRUE MALE FACTOID: Men are more uncomfortable with one-night stands than we are! Although men may want it, and be happy to engage in it, too much contact too soon spooks them. He'll feel like he just got married in a blackout and want a quick emotional annulment! He hears the cage door slamming and will try to teach you both a lesson . . . that he didn't really mean it (yet). Unless you only want him as a lover, slow him down before you pull his zipper down.

The Frequent Flyer
Is He Pathologically Incapable of Nesting,
Or Just Really, Really Busy?

Frequent Flyer's are very hip to their dysfunction. Trust me. Any time I've dated one of these troublemakers, he breaks the bad news right up front. On a first date, he'll typically say: "The last time I was in a serious relationship, my girlfriend threw a hammer at my head! I've been single ever since."

After you date him for a while, you'll want to hit him in the head with a hammer, too.

Clue: All his exes are nuts/psychos/stalkers! Of course, a Frequent Flyer would find someone he was justified in running away from, or he'd have to admit that *he's* the problem.

Now, commitment-phobe's know that there's something wrong with them. The problem is, they're not usually willing to do anything to correct the problem, *or they'd be all better by now*. The real crazy-making part of this relationship will occur when you try to blow him off. Then he may start to fight for the relationship passionately

MAN FACT: *A commitment-phobic man won't commit to stepping up, or breaking up. Breaking up would be a commitment, too!*

When confronted with losing you, he'll try to buy time, so that he can "figure things out."

WARNING: Unless he's figuring it out with a therapist, he's going to keep concluding that women suffocate him, and quickly bugger off again.

You'll probably be the one who calls it quits once you get clear about his chronic flight addiction. For the record, I think that true commitment phobia is rare. Usually the men who we thought were terrible flight risks weren't quite ready to settle down yet.

They'll commit somewhere down the road, just not to us. Thank God, because that'll be ten years from now. By then, he'll be forty-five with the relationship skills of a fifteen-year-old and ready to work a relationship out with a twenty-two-year-old.

I'm sure you'll be married with children by then, or having sex with strapping youngsters yourself, and will have forgotten all about him!

"Is He a Flight Risk?" Checklist

D.I.Y. quiz to see if you're dating a commitment-phobe.

	YES	NO
Can't step up	___	___
Can't break up	___	___
Can't say the word we	___	___
Tenses when touched in public	___	___
Introduces you as his "friend"	___	___
Pretends he's allergic to your cats	___	___
Refers to his divorce as the happiest day of his life	___	___
Doesn't own pets	___	___
If he has plants and they're still living, he has a gardener	___	___
Made plans to spend Christmas without you	___	___
Buys you a T-Shirt for Valentines Day	___	___
Doesn't go on vacations with you	___	___
Has girlfriend replacement gadgets, like massage chairs, personal assistants, chefs and maids	___	___

Tip: If you've checked yes to three or more questions, buy handcuffs.

The F.U.Gitive
(aka Vagrant Migration)

The F.U.gitive is like The Terminator.* His hostility just keeps re-booting. His behavior is deeply passive-aggressive and is definitely meant to hurt you. He's the bastard who stands you up for Christmas at your parents' house, leaves you standing at the altar, or picks a fight the day before you're planning to go on vacation and flies the coop without you.

The F.U.gitive is manipulative. He picks an irrational fight to distract you from whatever plot he's hatching. This decoy fight is designed to keep you spinning and to distract you from whatever betrayal he's really planning (like sleeping with a bridesmaid in the cloakroom before your sister's wedding). Then, unbelievably, he'll excuse his behavior by blaming it on you. "Well, if you hadn't been such a downer, I wouldn't have had to sleep with her in the first place! I've decided to only sleep with women who act like they like me."

This tactic is designed to make him feel better about pulling the romantic rug out from under you. But he won't really feel bad about it one way or the other. After all, he's not the one getting screwed over, you are. F.U. gitives are dangerous predators who tear off into a sky full of gathering cumulus clouds and ominous thunder. A very heavy rain is sure to follow (your tears!)

If a man exhibits this kind of dastardly behavior more than once, put him in total isolation for life with no chance of parole. He is damaged goods and a hardened romantic criminal. Drop him from the flock and quickly put his head on the chopping block.

MANHANDLING MANEUVER: Stop hoping and start hating! Sometimes hate can be healing, too.

---

*The original, not the sequels.

twenty -one

The Secret Male Language Decoder

The following bird calls are typical of the easily startled modern male. Whether you've been with him for two weeks, two months, or two years, use this decoder to translate what he's actually saying when he utters the following phrases.

"I'll call you . . . tomorrow." Translation: "I want to get off the phone now."

"I'll call you soon." Translation: Unfortunately, we have noway of determining the meaning of this with to-day's current technology.

"I'm fine." Translation: "Please shut up or change the subject."

"No problem." Translation: "I heard you. You can stop talking now."

"No, really, that looks great on you!" Translation: "If I tell you the truth, you won't blow me tonight."

"I'll help you in a minute." Translation: "Go ahead and do it yourself."

"I'll call you." Translation: "I'm not calling you until I start lusting after livestock."

"I need some space." *Translator's Note:* Meaning is completely dependent upon how totally you've managed to piss him off. *Translation:* (1) "I want to temporarily break up with you and have sex with my secretary." (2) "Back off! You're pressuring me and I'm teaching you a lesson." (3) "We're breaking up."

"I feel trapped." *Translation:* "Get off my back, woman!"

"I need space, I feel trapped." *Translation:* "We are breaking up right now. And don't forget to take your Tampax with you."

"I love you, but I'm not 'in love' with you." *Translation:* "I'll sleep with you, but you've been demoted to booty call status."

"I'm not looking for a relationship." *Translation:* "I'm not looking for a relationship with *you*. But we can have sex together until I find someone I decide to fall in love with."

"I'm enjoying my freedom right now." *Translation:* "I just dumped my girlfriend and I'm having the time of my life. But I'll be happy to put you into romantic rotation for a little workout!"

"I'm polyamorous." *Translation:* I just got out of a long marriage and am on a sexual spree! But if I fall in love with you, I'll probably get wildly jealous."

"I'm dominant" *Translation:* "No, I doesn't mean that I'm rich and want to get married. I just wanna Christian Grey you for free (without the shopping sprees and private planes). Who has that kind of cash?!"

"I don't want to get married." Translation: "I don't want to get married to *you*. But I'll be happy to date you until you start bringing up marriage, and then I'll remind you that we had this conversation and I won't feel guilty because it's your fault you didn't believe me when I told you I didn't want to get married to you" *(See Secret Male Lemon Law Disclaimer, page 61.)*

"I don't want children." Translation: "Whoa, slow down, are you kidding? I don't even own plants!"

"It's not you, it's me." Translation: "It's definitely you, trust me. I just don't want to go through the aggravation of discussing it and getting you even more pissed off at me."

"It's not me, it's you." Translation: "It's definitely me, but I'll try to keep the audition process going as long as possible until you get wise and finally dump me."

"Let's hang out." Translation: Has a variety of meanings:(1) I really like you." (2) "You're a booty-call." (3) "I'm not sure if I'm really attracted to you, so let's hang out and see what happens."

"Let's hook up." Translation: "Don't expect too much, 'cause I'm too cheap or too blasé about you to bother spending money on you. But we can definitely have sex if you want to!"

"I like you as 'a friend." Translation: "I definitely don't want to have sex with you (right now)."

"Later, dude." Translation: "I do not, will not, and cannot think about you in a sexual way. EVER."

"I love you." Translation: Correctly interpreting the meaning of this phrase is completely event-dependent:

DURING SEX: "I love having sex with you."

DURING A FIGHT: "I'm trying to distract you from the fact that I slept with your best friend."

FIRST THING IN THE MORNING: "Seriously, I really, really love you."

*"**Oh Christ, I love you!!**" Translation:* "Thanks for swallow-ing"

MAN FACT: *When you ask a man what he's thinking about and he says, "Nothing," he usually means it. Men, like Neanderthals, are often simply watching the fire and scratching their balls.*

Bizarre Birdcalls
Keeping (Phone) Tabs on Their Prey

Have you ever noticed that men seem to know exactly when you've stopped thinking about them and then, suddenly, they call? Your heart contracts. Or flips. Or stops. How did he know that you were almost free and then magically call you at that very moment?

I have discovered that men have an internal tracking system that allows them to calculate how long it will take for you to recover from whatever damage they've inflicted and crawl out of harm's way. Then they call you up to see if their talons (hooks) are still in. This is a genetic holdover from their cavemen days when their day job was hunting, wounding, and killing big furry bison.

Or they're psychic. Nah! I'm gonna go with the Internal Prey Escape Meter.

You Haven't Heard a Peep

Dear God, let the phone ring.
It would be such a little, little thing, just RING!!
—Dorothy Parker

He suddenly dropped out of sight and you haven't heard a peep. There is nothing quite as maddening as waiting for a call from an errant lover on the wing. You go from anticipation to hope to worry to anger, and then manage to talk yourself back into hope all over again. You wonder if you should call him. Maybe he's ill, or in trouble . . . *or maybe he got hit by a bus?!*

Romantic Rule: *If a man isn't calling you, it means that he doesn't want to talk to you!*

At least not right now. But he'll call the second he pulls his head out of his ass. Wait him out. Back away from the phone and delete his number so you won't be tempted to call him on a whim. Trust me. Men always call again if they really care about you. Hopefully, you'll be happily dating a hot stud at the time and answer his call with a nonchalant "Hey, what's up, Brosif? Long time no speak."

Relationship expert Pat Allen says that you should accept the fact that a man has totally flown the coop if you haven't heard from him within two months. He's still a viable prospect if he calls within eight weeks, however, so don't fret! If there is a temporary communication blackout, he may be trying to wrap his head around the idea of stepping up and seriously dating you, or tying up a loose end, named Susan. So wait him out and give him his space. And until then, get thyself on Tinder!

Romantic Rule: *If he's really falling for you, he'll call to "check in" within two months tops. Or right after he breaks up with his Aryuvedic massage therapist.*

The Come-and-Go Caller

Always beware the man who has sex with you and doesn't call the following day. He's distancing himself from you and the intimacy of the act, and he's sending you a very clear message: "Don't expect anything from me. I'm going to try to get away with calling whenever I feel like it, and if you fall for it . . . why, that'd be perfect! I'd be delighted to have sex with you again."

So remember: After you've had sex, carefully observe his phone patterns for important phone clues of ongoing consistency, unless all you wanted was that sexy Jaybird's booty-call in the first place.

> **MANHANDLING MANEUVER:** When he finally does call, let his message go straight to hell (voicemail). Listen to his excuse, and then return it several (this means at least two) days later, if you so choose. He doesn't deserve any more enthusiasm from you than what he's *so* not showering you with. Respect thyself!

ODD Romantic Rule: When your mirror a man's lack of interest he'll often totally change his tune.

When his distancing trick doesn't work the way it normally should (making you feel insecure so that you'll be over eager to rebook him), he may start to hunt you down. We teach men how to treat us, so educate him thusly: *"You seemed a little too blasé for me. George. Maybe we could get together and go bowling."* Any man willing to show up after hearing a line like this is worth giving a second chance to!

You Haven't Heard a Peep
(aka the Wild Blue Yonder Caller)

It's been more than two months since he was on your radar and he calls you right out of the blue. What's a girl to do?

Options: If you choose to answer this call out of curiosity, the tone to hit is one of friendly detachment: *"Well, hello Howard, what's up?"*

Critical Tip: DO NOT FLIRT!

1. He's transitioning you from leading lady to a friend, and enough time has passed for this to occur.
2. He just cleared his romantic roster and wants romantic or sexual re-engagement.
3. "Plan A" with an MVP fell through and he needs a date replacement.
4. He wants his leather jacket back.
Note to self: Make a trip to the Salvation Army.
5. He truly misses you and wants to take another shot at it.

Callback Rules for the
"Wild Blue Yonder Caller"

Stay Alert: Conduct this experiment in pristine conditions so as not to contaminate the results with a false positive. This may be the only (golden) opportunity to release yourself from the bondage of obsessing about this Nemesis Bird for the rest of your life.

1. Never ask him out.
2. Don't ask him where he's been.
3. Keep the conversation light and polite.

Be upbeat and share great news, like your promotion or closing escrow on a new home. Let him know that your life is *great*. Remember, he is not a friend, he's your Nemesis Caller!"

4. End the phone call first, and if he asks you out, heads up: It's a romantic do-over!

Fighting on the Phone

It is always unwise to fight with a man over the phone. There is no way to kiss and make up! If you're angry, let his call go straight to VM until you're calmer. You won't be put on the spot and will gain valuable time to regain your composure. Your temporary silence will speak volumes to a man. You are now speaking to him in his own language (space and timely withdrawal), and he will definitely get the message. Besides, re-corded bird-songs, yield tons of information, so listen carefully to his message for important clues . . . like an apology!"

MANHANDLING MANEUVER: *Let your voicemail do the talking!*

Know When to Be Unavailable

Always screen the following:

A man who returns your call or e-mail three days to one week later. Translation: You are not a priority! (This one's easy to understand, but may hard to accept.) He can't get nailed for being rude, but he is now con-tacting you in a way that is devoid of urgency."

Romantic Rule: *Remember, if there is no urgency, then nature isn't calling him urgently, and that spells trouble for romance.*

The Late-Night Caller. Don't respond to a man's calls or texts after 9 p.m. unless you're already dating, or he's taking you to Hawaii. Otherwise, screen him, and call him back during the light of day, to prevent getting a "Sext."

The Avoidance Caller. This crazy maker calls and leaves messages when he knows you won't answer your phone, like when you're perfoming surgery in the E.R.

What a clever bird! Take out your cleaver. Snap.

A man who demotes you from physical contact, to digital. A man who loves you will want to hear the sound of your voice, hold you in his arms, and see you *in person.* He won't be satisfied communicating with you via electronic media, alone.

1. If a man lives in your neighborhood, he should call you on the phone and definitely make speedy plans to meet you in person. Long delays are almost always red flags, and often a telltale sign that he's probably dating other women, and has put you on the back burner. (Ouch!)

2. If he used to call you and starts just texting you instead, you're being demoted. This is a distancing technique and signals that he is stepping back without totally letting you go. You are now in romantic rotation. Position: benched. *Tip:* Get out of the dugout!

3. Remember: If a man keeps it strictly virtual, he's a virtual waste of your time. Don't allow phone calls or text messages to become "date replacements." Talk for five minutes tops and then hop off the phone first, by saying: "Well, it was so great hearing from you. Thanks for calling, but my soup's almost done!" That'll be a clue that you're not just up for idle chit-chat.

WARNING: Men who keep it strictly "virtual" (and never make plans to meet you in person) are just cheating on their wives.

Knock Him Off His Virtual Perch

The Virtual Boyfriend is the most likely to turn tail, and if his texts get too racy (and too soon!), here's how to quicky lower the boom . . . Just text him this: "Dear Maxwell, I only text like that with men I'm currently dating. But I appreciate your enthusiasm!" and he'll knock it off!

Lovescript to get him to call you the phone, to make a first date; This modern phenomena of men just texting and not calling to set up a first date is something that every selfrespecting woman needs to know how to manhandle.

What to do with a Virtual Romeo. When men send you reams of texts but don't make plans to meet you from dating apps, they are a literal waste of time. You'd be better off spending your time playing computer poker. To get him to bust a move, just text him this: "Perhaps a chat on the phone would be lovely?" You might be surprised that he'll try to call you, *pronto!*

The Upside: The screens out Wingnuts.

Romantic Rule: *Never agree to go on a first date with a CyberSuitor unless he agrees to give you a ring on the phone, first!*

Always talk (aka screening or vetting) your new man on the phone, before you agree 'where and when' to meet him in person: Holding firm to this rule will end most (bad) first dates before they ever begin, became once he does call, you'll find out if he's someone worth schlepping out to meet, in person. When you chat with a man and hear the sound of his voice, you'll get a ton of info that you can't get via text, (like his intelligence level, your conversational "flow" and if he's easy to make plans with, etcetera), *Perk:* It's easier to break a date with a woman when he hasn't connected (met yet or really *talked* to), and this will prevent you from getting stood up, burnt-out, and Ghosted.

Odd Fact: Women often give me push-back on this! But I am right on this point, and if you are getting burnt-out by accepting lame dates, you'll thank me later for this time-saving advice.

If you don't feel that "click," and he's a dud, you can easily wrap up the call with this catchy conversation killer; *"Gee, my dinner's burning on the stove, but thanks for chatting, and have a fabulouse a night!"* and just hop off the line! (Umm, you're using a burner number for dating apps, right? Good girl! I was just checking!)

And if you've already met him in person, and are currently dating, when you want him to give you a call, just text him this. *"I'd love to hear the sound of your voice …"* and he'll get the message. And you'll get his call!

twenty-two

Has Your Relationship Gone to the Birds

Stuffing the Bird

Most women love to fluff up everything around them. My calico cat was the recipient of much (unwanted) attention. He never asked to be put in a dolly dress, and in one photo is struggling with a cherry lolly that I rammed into his mouth "because he liked it." The bunny got sent to the vet when I "accidentally" hugged it too hard, (he lived), and I broke my Easy-Bake Oven from excessive entertaining.

I, like so many women, needed to overcome the tendency of getting carried away by *the activities* associated with being "in love." This is dangerous territory to tread on, especially in the courtship phase of a relationship. (Stick to bikini waxing, jogging, and dust busting.) Unfortunately, when you become a whirling dervish of romantic activity, you run the risk of stifling your suitor's natural instinct to ante up and build the relationship *with* you. Men are practical. If you're doing all of the hard labor, they'll take it as a cue to move their focus to other important things (like Foosball), because in their minds . . .you're handled.

Don't give more time, energy, or attention to the men you're dating than they're giving back to you. Remember: Men fall in love through the process of doing. They need to build a nest around you to mark their territory and to make the relationship their own. If you're always one step ahead of them, they'll feel unappreciated, unnecessary, and even emasculated. This dynamic will not result in the torrid sex that you deserve!

Romantic Rule: Overgiving short-circuits the male coupling instinct! If your man has become romantically lazy, it's probably because your overabundant giving has drowned his desire to win and woo.

When you're stuck in quicksand, the more you do, the deeper you'll sink. At this juncture many women sink even deeper by mistakenly thinking that they're not doing enough to please their man. In a panic, they redouble their winsome efforts in a misguided attempt to revive his ardor and attention.

The only way to get unstuck is to stop acting like Santa in a mini. When he finally calls you again (and trust me, they almost *always* call again), let him take *you* out to dinner, let *him* pick up the check, and let him give *you* head. The only thing you're allowed to do is enjoy yourself, and the only things you're allowed to say are "A little to the left," "Yes, right there!" and "Thank you!"

Over giving creates guilt, not marriage. Most men believe in the scales of justice and don't want to be characterized as being selfish or unfair. The biggest reason not to overgive is because it makes your man feel guilty. He'll only wind up feeling manipulated by racking up a romantic debt that's not of his

MAN FACT: *Men are professionals at keeping score!*

Most men secretly enjoy jumping through hoops of fire, scaling craggy cliffs, and bringing over Chinese takeout. But if you tip the scales of romantic justice and burden a man with a love debt, it will ultimately backfire. Usually, the trouble begins when you notice that he's not really reciprocating in kind.

Many women will now start to make the classic mistake of complaining about everything they've been doing *for* him. Who asked you to teach his children French anyway? (You!) This is a terrible way to get your man to make a deeper commitment, and you risk violating the supreme rule of male courtship: **Men only do what they want to do.**

No matter what men say, watch what they do. When you "stuff the bird" men construe it as pressure, and a big reaction is sure to follow. Over giving can induce *La-Z-Boy Recliner Syndrome* or turn a Lovebird into a Bat Out of Hell. If the gods really want to punish you for poor manhandling, you might even wind up with six feet of trouble. He's the type who'll be more than happy to sit in your nest and channel surf until you come home from a hard day at the office, and expect you to cook him dinner!

Instead, when you wisely pull back, men will naturally pick-up the slack and romantically reengage *if they're good partners for you.* And you'll have given yourself the priceless gift of clarity. You might need to make changes in how you choose to prioritize your relationship!

Tip: Low self-esteem and 'fear of loss' are the biggest reasons women overcompensate with men, in the first place. And then wind up putting themselves in second place! It 'll be easy to see what your partner's contributing once you've stepped back, and given the fella some breathing room. You'll see what you've got left on your plate, and then you can "deal with the meal" that he's *serving.*

Romantic Rule: *Slim Jim's and Hershey's Kisses are not a balanced dinner. Stop grazing!*

Circling Your Pray
Help for the Chronically Obsessed

Do you obsessively think about "him" and "your relationship"? Here's now to snap yourself out of the hypnotic state you've put yourself into, by "circling your prey."

Romantic Rule: *No one is obsessed when their needs are fully met, unless their heart's been "wounded."*

This is a bad state of affairs, and it's going to take a little looking into . . .

The "Are you Obsessed" Test
A helpful checklist

	YES	NO
Do you go to sleep thinking about him?	___	___
Do you wake up in the middle of the night thinking about him?	___	___
Do you wake up in the morning thinking about him?	___	___
Do you talk about him incessantly?	___	___
Introduces you as his "friend"	___	___
Do you make new friends so that you can talk about him some more?	___	___
Do you talk about him to total strangers and hair-stylists?	___	___
Do you wake up in the morning thinking about him?	___	___
Do you talk about him incessantly?	___	___
Do you call the psychic hot-line and talk to the dead about him?	___	___
Do you talk to spirits through tarot and the I Ching to divine his "inner thoughts"? (This actually works!)	___	___
Do you qualify to become a detective because of your covert sleuthing?	___	___
Do you Google him obsessively?	___	___

If you answered "Yes!" to more than three of the above questions, you're "Officially Obsessed."

Breakup & Make-Up Addiction

Well, he dumped you. You weren't that into him during the courtship, but now all you want in the *whole wide world* is to get him back. You'll do anything because your bruised ego is pushing you beyond all reason.

Note: This is not love, it's personal!

The uncertainty about when you'll actually see him is part of the allure of this relationship, and anxious tension super-charges each encounter with too much INTENSITY. You feel like you're lovers reuniting after a war. (*See Cold Mountain*). You might compulsively call him and persist in heart-wrench-ing conversations,(ie. *Where did you meet that brunette? How old is she? Twenty-three?!*). Finally, you might even resort to calling and hanging up, texting, and of course, social media stalking—and take a shot at knocking on his door in your linge-rie, (without any warning).

Symptoms: Engaging in lots of makeup and break sex.

The Upside: Mascara streaks on cheeks really do give you a sexy punk rock look! You're pretty darned irresistible!

Revenge Obsession:
(aka Tormenting Your Prey)

Now you're having sex *at* him, not *with* him.

Fact: Revenge sex is often better than make-up sex, breakup sex, and even middle-of-the-night wake-up sex, but it's very bad manners! So only do it if you *really, really want to.*

Consequence: Operatic over-the-top DRAMA!! This is only good if you're very bored and have no personal responsibilities, like work, pets, or plants; are independently wealthy; and know karate. Because he is going to want to strangle you after you have sex with his business partner, brother, or best friend, or try to get him deported, or put Nair in his shampoo. Revenge obsession is not only time-consuming, (even though at the time it seems fun), and is de-stabilizing and ultmately, utterly demoralizing. This is called *"lowering the tone"* and is not good etiquette! It has, however, been practiced by all the best families. (*See* The Tudors, the Scots, and the Medicis.)

The Gone With the Wind - Love Addict

You refuse to accept that this man does not, will not, or cannot return your affections. You stupidly pass up opportunities for true love because you're still carrying a torch for someone who has no real romantic interest in you. The torch that you're carrying is actually there to light the terrible darkness you're in. Girl, you're so stubborn, you must be a Taurus!

Problem: You are someone capable of mistaking friendship and sexual attraction with love. And it's easy to do when men are so darned attractive to *you.* Another way to describe this is Romantic Narcissism.

Case Study:
Scarlett O'Hara, Love Addict

Scarlett O'Hara is the poster child of all women living in obsession driven denial. I interviewed her last spring, and although she's still not in recovery, I'm thrilled to report that she's taking great delight in tormenting all of the men at the Twelve Oaks Retirement Home.

ME: So, Scarlett, what's become of your Captain Butler?
SCARLET: That ancient history? I got over that silly crush! . .
. Oh, and good morning to you, Morris! Don't you look handsome in your new blue cardigan. Why, yes, I'd be delighted to
sit next to you at Bingo . . . I'm sorry, what were you saying?
ME: Captain Butler? Are you still in touch?
SCARLET: Well, I went to Charleston to surprise him that
onetime. But we're taking a little break right now. Did he ask
about me?
ME: Um . . . Not exactly.
SCARLET: Oh, let's talk about something else. [Pause] Oohh-
hh, look at that fat old India Wilkes. Isn't her dress just awful? I
wouldn't be caught dead in it!

WARNING: Attention to women who date unavailable men:
It's time to Get Woke.

If you've set your sights on an unavailable man, or worse, one
who isn't even on the same page as you (you're stuck on page
22), but he's closed the book, or worse, thrown it at you!, here's
a tip: T-H-ER-A-P-Y. Consider it. If you're not sure you're obsessed, call three of your closest friends and ask them if they
think you're in danger of "being tragic" in the Victorian sense
of the word, as in waiting for your soldier to come back from
the Prussian War kind of tragic.

Fashion Tip: This kind of drama only looks fantastic in a
hoop skirt. Unchecked, this kind of thing can go on for years.
The good news is that you have a fabulous imagination! It will
finally be put to excellent use if you decide to deprogram yourself . . .

Become a Member Of
The Mind Police

When you change your actions, your thoughts and feelings
will ulitmately *follow.* The following seven steps are fabulous
aids to help you release yourself from any obsessive love spell.

1. ***Deprogram Yourself.*** Delete his phone number from
your cell phone, Unfriend him on Facebook and stop following him on social media, and of course, delete him from your

inbox on Bumble, Hinge or Match.

2. *Change your habits.* Instead of driving by his house after yoga, find an alternate route. *Tip:* It takes ninety days to break or create a new habit. Mark it on your calendar, and then have a cupcake! It'll make you feel great.

3. *Rubber band snapping.* Put a large rubber band around your wrist and snap it hard every time you think about him. It will reveal how much energy you've been wasting on him and it's also amost as painful.

4. *Recite the alphabet backward.* This is very hard to do and will make it impossible to obsess about him—or anything else for that matter, so don't put on false eyelashes or operate heavy machinery when practicing this technique.

5. *Visualize a STOP* sign every time you think about him.

6. *Practice aversion therapy visualizations* Imagine that he's got a terrible case of the crabs! And every time you long for his magic wand, imagine him reaching into his pants and scratching away like a dog with fleas.

7. *Try actual therapy, and get complete with your past***!** (This really does work.)

And when all else fails, just try . . .

8. *The Dick Replacement Program.* Have sex with men you can't take seriously, because they're so hot, but wayyyy too young or dumb to love.

This is fun, effective, the perfect way to get over the hump, and is *such a boon* for them.

Love is like musical chairs. It's up to you how long you stay out of the game after the music has stopped. When you're ready to find love, just start dating again!

twenty-three

Flipping the Bird

Surprisingly enough, most men polled suggested that instead of blowing them off, women should just blow them, although this, too, could lead to some very hard feelings!

—Lauren Frances

Empty Nesters

You recently broke up and can't stand the loneliness. You're used to having a man in your bed! When a woman rushes back into the wilds, however, she may often wind up with some strange birds in her nest. This can send her even further into a slough of despondency (dating depression). What's a girl to do?

This may be the perfect time to consider the "recyclable male."

Have Sex with an Ex

This is the "magic doorway" where ex-lovers can get back in. Sometimes its not only the *nice* thing to do, it's the right thing to do! Let's examine some options:

The Puddle Jumper. You call him and cry on his shoulder every time you break up. He spoons you, which is even more tragic than being alone because you just sort of lie there. He's the always-there guy, but for some reason you never take him seriously. He's so *nice*. Too nice, in fact. Hello! Maybe you try the "Kiss Test" and if it's hot, then marry him!

And then again, there's always Sven. Sometimes I find that having a lover named Sven really expedites my emotional healing. Although some may dismiss this as "hot rebound sex," it can really perk you up! When grieving, many women love having a romp, or just making-out! If you're afraid you'll forget their names, just call 'em "Superman" or "Handsome!"

Stick a Fork In It

Sometimes when women break up, they don't want to *stay* broken up, (aka Relationship Recidivism). This is because most of us are true romantics and have an aversion to an *unhappy ending*. This state of affairs (sad!) often occurs when you won't close the book on a dead-end relationship and refuse to write "The End" because you don't like the way that your love story turned out.

Problem: Your hope is like watering leaves that have fallen off trees. You break up repeatedly, then get back together, then breakup all over again, but never quite close the door on this relationship. If you're one of the many women who can't break off a dead-end love affair, I have one word for you: Closure. And here's a fun way to get it . . .

Stage a Relationship Funeral

Invite your Mantrap Pack and closest friends. You know, the gals whose shoulders are damp with your tears, (and are secretly thrilled that you've finally rid yourself of that rat bastard, so they can go on living their lives without worrying about you tearing out your hair. But they're true blue friends, and say say comforting things, like: "He's such a loser/ idiot/narcissist/fuckwit!" and "You'll definitely find someone better!" and "You're skin looks just amazing, by the way." "We're going out on the town. Seriously! No one can tell you've been crying. "

Relationship Funeral Sample Script

As the scene opens, we pan in and see Marci's Mantrap Pack dressed completely in black. Candles are lit. Macabre music plays in the background.

> "Dearly Beloved, we are gathered today to mourn the passing of Stacy and Jonathan's relationship. There was a lot of great sex, hot dates, and verbal banter. And that trip to Guam. Didn't you get terrible food poisoning there, Stacy?
>
> (She nods).
>
> Alissa: That was probably a sign.
>
> ManTrap Pack: Yep! Mmm hhhhmmm. Aha.
>
> Alissa: Unfortunately, this relationship was dead on arrival last April, but Stacy kept it alive by tube feeding, selfless booty calling, intense prayer, and frequent drive-by's. Stacy, would you like to say a few words?

Stacy: Well, yes, yes, I would. [Sniff.] Jonathan, as you all know, was a just a terrible skirt chaser. I totally deserve to be with someone who is truly available, steadily employed, and who wants to chase only one skirt . . . mine. But I did love him and will miss the way he used to talk in his sleep and played fetch with my cat. It was damned cute! [Hiccup.]

ManTrap Pack: Remember when he got ass rash? Ewww!"

MANHANDLING MANEUVER: *You may also choose Bonfire Therapy as an alternative. Take significant mementos of your relationship, like vacation photos, concert ticket stubs, and his vintage Led Zeppelin T-shirt, and cremate them in your fireplace, or put them in a shoe box and bury it in the backyard. I'm a proponent of bonfire therapy myself, but that's just me.*

(Stacy's Mantrap Pack even helped her make a cardboard tombstone! Fun!)

The Burial

Jonathan & Stacy
July 4, 2017, to June 28, 2019
Rest in peace*

THE END

Alissa leads the group in a solemn prayer:
*"Ashes to ashes,
Dust to dust.
Now that you're free,
A martini's a must!"*

And they quickly adjourn to a local bar to celebrate!

* (Or pestilence . . . it's up to you!)

Romantic Rule: When you're having difficulty letting go of a relationship, stick a fork in it.

Helpful Thoughts
When Your Goose Is Cooked:

- If he were such a great guy, you'd still be with him.

- If he's making you feel this bad, he's not "the One."

- Their rejection is God's protection.

- You can't do the wrong thing in the right relationship.

- You can't do anything right in the wrong one.

- Your love counts even if your relationship didn't work out.

- Staying in resentment is like drinking poison and hoping that the other person dies.

- Poor me, poor me, pour me a drink!

twenty-four

The Pterodactyl

Are you getting hexed by your ex? If a ghost from your past is endangering your romantic future, it's time to do some spring cleaning ...

The Pterodactyl is the extinct lover, the one you're now convinced was really *"the One." Problem:* He either dumped you or died, or you stupidly broke up with him for reasons that now, in hindsight, seem completely insane. And although you're no longer together (in this dimension), you can't quite manage to break up with him *in your mind.*

The Pterodactyl prevents us from being with living, giving, and available men. Rather than risk another possible heartbreak, victims of the past often stop dating altogether or become overly critical of new suitors. You see nothing but their faults and silently measure them against what could now be diagnosed as a Holy Grail–like obsession with how perfect he was.

In a truly honest moment, you'd probably admit that the only reason he seems so perfect is because he's not here. He can't leave his filthy gym socks on your white duvet cover or annoy you in the myriad of ways that real mortals do because he's othersise engaged or has moved to France.

In fact, if you think *really* hard, you might even remember why you broke up with him in the first place. It was probably because he had some fatal deal-breaking flaw that you couldn't live with no matter how hard you tried.

Clues You're Living with a Pterodactyl

- You're still wearing his T-shirt to bed.

- When you spend quality time with your vibrator, his name comes up.

- The phrase "get back out there" makes you vomit in your mouth.

- You fear that close friends are screening your calls.

- You're wearing the engagement ring on your right hand or have craftily strung it on a chain around your neck.

- Or (this is serious) you're still wearing the diamond on your ring finger!

WARNING: Pterodactyls hang about, because we haven't properly mourned their passing. They are common sightings in the lives of many lovely, lonely women and they need to be cast out! If your heart is obscured by a past relationship, swift action will need to be taken to walk you back into present time.*

Exorcising the Pterodactyl

He may be married to someone else, living upstate with a brood of five, or planted six feet under. Whatever his excuse, one thing's for certain: He's not here, and in all likelihood, won't be coming back to roost with you again in this in carnation.

Attempting to exorcise the Pterodactyl unaided can be an arduous task. Many women are so plagued by repeat visitations that they're doubtful that they'll ever be free to love again. You may have even built up an entire mythology around him and keep paying psychic homage to a dead relationship as a way of keeping some thin connection alive. Like me, you've probably watched one too many episodes of the movie *Ghost.* Please remember that when you're haunted, it's hard to want to jump into Cyberspace. You'd rather watch netflix alone at your place.
But it's not good to stay in that headspace too long!

---

* Keeping skeletons in your closet doesn't leave enough room for your Christian Louboutin shoes!

Tip: Refrain from having long conversations with people who aren't actually in the room with you. Stop chatting with about your sexy ghosts with anyone who'll listen (after a year or two!) Everyone knows that if you keep talking about them, they'll keep hanging about. Love phantoms are bored, and giving them your time and attention is like wearing Lovescript perfume around well-dressed frenchmen.

Maria Callas wound up alone after Ari, even though she was magnificent. (Google it.)

You'll never be free of your Pterodactyl until you can accept the cold hard fact that it's over. It's time to accept defeat and embrace the white flag of surrender.

Decide to go into "focused mourning" for 30 days, max.

The Upisde: Everyone looks great wearing black! Unleashing pent-up feelings will break your (dry) spell. Don't miss any-opportunity to cry in restaurants, re-read love letters, write your "Love Story" as a Ghost Story, and then burn it out back. And then try on all of the great outfits that I know you've got stashed away in your lingerie drawer. It'll always help you get right back on track!

To Un-Hex Your Heart. Shut your door, light a candle, and pay close attention. We are going to make a "revulsion amulet" to keep your seductive Romantic Vampire at bay.

The Amnesia List

To dispel unwanted "visitations," get a pen and *make a list of every single irritating thing* that you can remember about your Pterodactyl. Make sure to write down *everything;* from horrible character flaws (like when you met his ex and he "forgot" to introduce you) to bad habits, (he liked to floss and talk). Yink! You can expand this list to include the pros and cons of the relationship, but in truth, you would probably be better served by a solid list of negatives. Here's an example:

Sample Amnesia List

• He could pronounce the work monodagomy, but had trouble defining it

•Foreply consisted of him ripping he foil off the condom package.

He didn;t pick you up at the airport when you flew ten hours to see him!

The answer to any "relationship" question was two weeks of the silent treatment.

• He has a tattoo on his hip that says, Trust No One.

• He always wore socks, even if sometimes that's all he was wearing.

• He bought tires for your birthday.

• He thinks that sneakers are shoes.

Keep this "revulsion amulet" with you at all times, no matter what. You can never tell when a love phantom will strike, so "better safe than sorry", as they say in France. It should fit nicely in your wallet or in the naughty nightstand drawer where you keep the condoms. And any time you find yourself humming his favorite song, or start to make out with him in your mind, whip out your Amnesia List instead, and read it all the way through. You'll remember all of the pain he caused you, and if all goes well, you'll be as appalled by his apparition as you would whilst bikini shopping underneath fluorescent lights at the mall.

This is like taking down your own Berlin Wall to love. Put away all photos and significant mementos of "him," until you get over the hump and are dating again. Shoe boxes tucked away in dark corners are the perfect resting place for love-tainted mementos, interestingly!

Don't wear the earrings he gave you for Christmas. Stop wearing his football jersey to bed. And please do away with that stuffed armadillo he brought back from that business trip to Texas.

But don't give away actual pets unless you don't like them, are allergic to them, or were only putting up with them because you were being a "good sport." It's perfectly find to give his pet hamster back.

MANHANDLING MANEUVER: Restrain yourself from mentioning him, especially when you're out on a date. You're boring everyone with this line of conversation anyway, and all it does is summon up your ghost.

Starving the Pterodactyl

If he's still physically hanging around, or calling just to be *"friendly"* (to keep you on the string), or, even worse, sleeping with you once in a blue moon, you must cease all contact with him for at least six months. That means no phoning, texting, snap chatting, liking his posts, and if you're old school, no birthday cards or faxes. If he doesn't respect your need for mental breakup space, add this to your Amnesia List!

Don't ask him to return your books, pillow, or wok. These are just lame excuses you've drummed up to stay in contact with him and he *knows* it. Don't try to rustle up any gossip about him or waste your time imagining what he's doing with . . . her. Instead, starve this ghost out of the landscape of your day-to-day mind and you'll make room for a brand-new love to fly in, *because it's time.*

Pray for the Bastard

The final key to Unhexing Your Yeart is to simply pray for the bastard. I don't know why this works. It just does. Try using this effective multipurpose prayer every day for two weeks, and just see what happens:

"Dear Lord, please let him get exactly what he deserves!"

This will free you from the negative feelings that are keeping you stuck in the past like psychic superglue. When you wish him well (a state of forgiveness), you free *yourself,* no matter how big of a dick that the prick was to you. This is exactly where you need to be (mentally) to find true love again. Promise you'll get out of the shadows, and back to the land of the living. Because Christmas, New Years, Valentine's Days not to mention birthdays, are more fun with a loving man in your bed, (and not just one that's gotten stuck in your head). So here's to having a new boyfriend by Thanskgiving, so let's go. It's time to rally, and Onward Ho!

Setting limits isn't rejection, it's correction!

*Men are very naughty sometimes, so
don't take any crap!*

—Lauren Frances

manhandling

part iii

twenty-five

Can You Train This Bird?

It is vital when you live with a pet that you learn how to train it. If your man struggles to maintain goodwill and good manners, he'll only cause you heartache! Always remember that the bird is the closest living thing to the dinosaur. Even in the happiest of relationships, your partner's ability to speak on command, maintain good indoor behavior, and be of good cheer when cooped up with you for extended periods of time will be *limited* at best. That's why every woman should have some manhandling techniques up her sleeve to make sure she doesn't get crapped on.

Romantic Rule: *You shouldn't be afraid of your pets, wonder where they are, or have to guess if they love you, too.*

Men need to put a woman's happiness *first* because most women naturally care for others without any coaching whatsoever. It's hard-wired into our DNA. That's why men need to prove, through their actions, that they're willing to care about your happiness as much as their own.

Your man will take cues from you about how you'd like to be treated, and to see what kinds of behavior he can or cannot get away with. If you accept bad behavior and refuse to set limits with him, you'll encourage him to just behave badly! To ensure that you don't saddle yourself with a selfish, unworkable, or obstinate man, you need to see if he cares enough about your relationship to shape up if he needs to, and will respond to your coaching.

Romantic Rule: The Goddess already knows that you'll take care of him. We need to make sure that he'll delight in taking care of you!

CPB: Cost Per Bird

Having a relationship shouldn't cost your peace of mind, self-respect, your family and friends who love you, or the special things that bring you joy. If you find that your CPB (cost per bird) is higher than your re-turns, the price you're paying is much too high. Just say, "Bye!"

Is he Teachable?

You won't know if you can effectively train a man until some kind of conflict arises. This "first fight" is a litmus test to evaluate your partnership potential. Conflicts are golden opportunities to find out a wealth of important information about your new friend. We want to see if he fights fairly.

Romantic Rule: This golden "first-fight" opportunity will present itself as a conflict of needs. It's like looking into a crystal ball and seeing your relationship's future.

The way that a man communicates during a disagreement gives you a sneak preview of his problem-solving skills and, more important, it speaks volumes about his character. You want a man who not only cares about your feelings, but actually *enjoys* taking care of them. If you find yourself with such a man, you are in luck. You've landed a top notch bird! His considerate behavior and responsiveness to your needs will build trust and a loving relationship. They are important clues that signal his capacity for successful pair bonding.

But if you find that your man's ego drives him to win at all costs, if he exhibits punishing behavior to make you submit to his will, or if he constantly flies into a rage, you've got trouble on your hands. Some men have never learned to coexist with a woman—or with another *human*, for that matter—and he's going to be a handful.

To Avoid Power Struggles

If your male exhibits Neanderthal-like behavior roughly 10 percent of the time, we consider this to be manageable bone headedness. But if he acts like a knucklehead more than 15 percent of the time, you have a discipline and maintenance problem on your hands. If unacceptable dominance or aggression is exhibited, it should be corrected in a calm but firm manner immediately.

- Be firm without being dominating or punishing.
- Use effective manhandling tools.
- Respect your pet.

FYI: He should not feel that filling your needs is an imposition, or an impossible and unpleasant task. Men should accommodate reasonable requests at all times unless they're ill, or watching a ball game.

twenty-six

Birdshit

Nipping Bad Behavior in the Bud

If you refuse to housebreak *your pet, you'll wind up with a mess.* Don't be a moving target! If your man continually exhibits aggressive or obnoxious behavior, ask yourself if it's something that you're willing to live with *for the rest of your life.* If you aren't, you must be willing to do what's necessary to remedy the situation. Then, with the patience of a saint and a backbone like Stalin's, decide on a course of action to retrain your bird. Consistency is key.

Manhandling requires self-discipline and self-sacrifice. If you want to train a man, you must be willing to re-train yourself, and change your own behavior *first.* Without self-discipline and introspection on your part, you'll never effect to change in him.

WARNING: When you change your behavior, you should expect a man to be miffed about his loss of status. He may scream, become peckish, or fly the coop temporarily. Don't be cowed by his behavior but take comfort in the fact that once he's housebroken, he'll be so much more fun to live with.

Romantic Rule: No man ever thanks you for setting boundaries with him. Especially when he needs it!

Limit Setting and the Modern Male

Men respond to actions, not words. They wrote the book on sweet talk, so they know instinctively that it's not what you *say,* it's what you do that counts. The most effective way to set boundaries with a man is to give him a time-out and take away privileges. In other words, real consequences for bad behavior.

Penalties are more effective than nagging and henpecking that he can easily tune out. If you're being treated disrespectfully, all of the conversation in the world won't change a man's rude behavior, but changing your actions certainly will! Let your behavior do the talking and show him exactly what naughty tricks won't be tolerated by you.

MAN FACT: *We teach people how to treat us. Men respond to actions, not words... unless you're talking dirty.*

Covering the Cage:
Boundary-Setting and Containment

Men who are emotionally healthy learn to contain themselves by taking a time-out when they're being hurtful to others. They take a break and then pop out of isolation once they've mastered their negative feelings.

Men who aren't self-aware don't know how to take a time-out and just terrorize everyone around them instead. This behavior is unacceptable and must be nipped in the bud. These men are tyrants and bullies. No amount of conversation with this little dictator will change his behavior one iota, but his fear of losing you may.

Romantic Rule: If his behavior is unacceptable, remove his favorite plaything. .. you!

The best thing to do when men misbehave is to give them a timeout, like you would with naughty children. To do this you'll have to contain your feminine desire to care take, over explain, and overshare your negative thoughts or feelings with him. A woman believes that if she expresses feelings of hurt, vulnerability, or upset, a man will automatically understand and even hug her (like her girlfriends certainly would). This thinking is so misguided. When men are angry, their blood is up and their instinct to cockfight is aroused, and they often just get mad.

It is not acceptable to hit, scream at, or henpeck your bird. Excessive punishment will only cause him to put up a terrible fuss, and he may become quite provoked and display overt hostility towards you.

Romantic Rule: *The best training for a bad bird to cover his cage and abandon the field. Dignified withdrawal is by far the best route to harmony.*

When a man behaves badly, excuse yourself, and stop talking. Don't reengage until after he's settled down. You may even have to physically leave the room if he won't stop fighting. When you let go of the rope, he'll wind up on his ass, and hopefully it'll knock some sense back into him.

He'll soon notice that his rights have been diminished, and he'll be forced to accommodate your needs or accept the alternative without you having to scream or fight with him about it.

Give Him an Altitude Adjustment

Altitude, or being Top Bird, is the primary goal of most men. Their place in the pecking order at work and at home is of vital importance to them. Men naturally seek the highest perch in a relationship (dominance), while women are more inclined to take other people's needs into consideration (I must pick berries and burp the baby, too).

MANHANDLING MANEUVER: *To train a naughty Parrot, instead of looking up at him on a branch above you, keep him situated so that his head is never higher than your heart. Take him down a notch! He needs to know that you're equals and that he won't remain king of the castle if he persists in foul behavior.*

For example, if you're constantly making trips to his house, ask him if he'll come to yours. Say, *"I'm too tired tonight. Would you please come my way, Scruffy?"* If he says, "No" (as we suspect he will), say, *"I'm disappointed but am going to stay home tonight. Sorry you don't want to join me. Guess I'll flip through my little black book and make a booty-call to my favorite Dodo."*

When your bird flies down from his perch and you're both seeing eye-to-eye once again, you may reward him as long as his behavior does not change accordingly.

Romantic Rule: Never put a man above your own heart.

Does Your Man Have an Attitude Problem?

	YES	NO
The relationship is on his terms.	____	____
He makes unreasonable demands for your time and attention.	____	____
He treats you like a second-class citizen.	____	____
Most of the sacrifices in the relationship come from you.	____	____
He puts his needs consistently above your own.	____	____
He takes you and the relationship for granted.	____	____

	YES	NO
He cops an attitude when you make reasonable requests of him.	____	____
He assumes that his point of view is always correct. He is overly critical of you.	____	____
He tries to bully or intimidate and criticize you, alone or in public.	____	____
He makes fun of you, even though he says he's only "joking."	____	____
He exhibits hurtful behavior that he refuses to change.	____	____
He is uncooperative and refuses to assist you in normal ways.	____	____

If you've answered "yes" to more than one item,
he needs to be taken down a notch immediately, hon!

MANHANDLING MANEUVER:
* *Stop waiting on him hand and foot.*
* *Stop speaking to him if he is rude to you.*
* *Restrict sexual playtime.*
* *If he's taking you for granted, pull back and take good care of yourself first.*
* *He needs to be on his knees for a while, and not the other way around.* *
* *No blow jobs!*

If this fails, we'll move on to lion-taming techniques. For this you'll need: a chair and whip . . .

Hmmm... maybe that's what he was after all along!

twenty-seven

Talk to the Animals

How to Talk to a Man When He's "Having a Feeling"

It may be hard to believe, but men have feelings, too. Their *"go-to"* feelings are quite different from ours, however. Men are often uncomfortable with weepy, vulnerable feelings, so their favorite upset feelings tend toward one of two kinds of anger: actively hostile (martial) or passive-aggressive (glacial).

Symptoms of active Anger Mode (macho) include raging about, throwing fits, irritation, meanness, shouting, curtness, sarcasm, aggression, and/or fisticuffs.

Symptoms of passive-aggressive Anger Mode (snotty) include eye rolling, face-making, withholding, silent treatment, pouting, groaning, sighing, disappearing, and/or sneaky plotting.

The best way to handle men when they're having a feeling, big or small, is to allow them to have it with minimal intervention. Step away when his feathers are ruffled and return once he's had time to settle down.

Often, you'll find that a man's "feelings" are triggered by the following:

Situational upset. Something happened to provoke a macho outburst of hostile feelings or bad behavior. It could be in response to an irritation with you, something at work, or a malfunctioning gizmo.

Male Attention Deficit Disorder, or M.A.D.D. It's a scientific fact: Men can only hear three sentences max before they start to tune you out. Anything over three sentences overloads them with too much information, causing men to panic, especially if the sentences are loaded with . . .

Heavy emotion (anger, tears, or both). This is liable to turn him into a Bat Out of Hell. He'll actively flee the scene of the emotional crime or go into an Emotional Coma. Strong emotions from you (any) actually cause him great alarm and trigger an inner defense system designed to shut him down, thus preventing and protecting him from an imminent threat (saying something stupid while you're crying and making things worse).When a man is in an Emotional Coma, he often becomes a Mute Swan and behaves as one temporarily incapable of speech. He, when pressed, may manage to grunt, "I'm sorry," or *"It's not my fault!"* Leave this bird alone! When men become mute, you have said enough. Many women repeat themselves,mistaking his silence for actual deafness.

MAN FACT: *He heard you. His brain just needs time to catch up!*

Upside to Men Suddenly Struck Mute: Men often place themselves voluntarily in (emotional) lock down by winging away, or falling mute, to stop themselves from bullying you or becoming overly aggressive.

Let him digest the information. In the meantime, get a manicure. When you return, see if he's figured out what you were trying to communicate before you left. If he pretends that nothing happened, try talking to him again without the waterworks, in three sentences max.

Let him respond or mull it over for a while now that he's heard you repeat it in a calmer tone.

Male (Emotional) A.D.D.
The Three-Sentence Rule

Scenario: You ask your man if you and he can *"talk."* About three sentences in, you notice that he's no longer talking or looking at you and, instead, has started playing a video game while nodding and grunting, *"Uh-huh. Hmm-mm-hhm."* You ask him to stop (whatever he's doing) and "talk" to you. He becomes ridiculously defensive that you've "accused him" of not paying attention and stalks out of the room.

Male A.D.D. usually occurs when a woman starts an unending stream of emotionally charged conversation. (Known in "Girl Speak" as *"communicating"* or *"sharing your feelings."*)

This is strangely misinterpreted by man-hearing, as *"nagging, bossing, and complaining."*

Female sharing often produces feelings of anxiety and panic in men, who respond to it by swiftly repositioning themselves to create a psychic buffer. They will then proceed to tune us out by doing something more productive, like playing computer poker.

MAN FACT: *Grunting and physically remaining in a room with a woman who's talking at him is considered "communicating" by most men.*

This is not a strategy, it is a primal urge that even the most metro sexual man possesses deep in his genetic hardwiring. This tune-out is such an old, yet effective, coping mechanism that it's impossible to reprogram.

The Three-Strikes-You're-Out Rule

The most effective way to talk to a man about a "hot topic" is to ambush him. By using the three-sentence rule you'll slip right under his radar. If you have to make a request of a man more than three times, you're not going to get what you need from him without a fight. At least not right now. You have struck out. Just accept it!

Most women do not know about this rule, and as a consequence, fall into the following trap:

Bungling the Three-Sentence Rule

Example: You're happily watching TV. Bob comes into the room, grabs the remote, and starts flipping the channels.

JESSICA: Bob, I would appreciate it if you didn't change the channel while I'm watching Masterpiece Theater.

BOB: [Grunts.] Umm-hmmm. [Continues to channel surf.]

JESSICA: Bob, it makes me feel disrespected when I make a request and you completely roll right over me.

BOB: [Silence, more channel surfing.] What?

JESSICA: Bob, would you please change the channel back?

BOB: Hang on.

JESSICA: Helloooooooo, Bob? Earth to Bob! BOB! ARE YOU DEAF?

BOB: You are such a nag! Here, watch whatever you want! [Tosses the remote control at Jessica and leaves the room in a huff.].

Romantic Rule: *When you get what you want by nagging, you still lose. If you repeat something more than three times, you're henpecking!*

Correct Use of the Three-Sentence Rule

JESSICA: Bob, I would appreciate it if you didn't change the channel when I'm watching Masterpiece Theater.

BOB: [Grunts.] Umm-hmmm. [Doesn't change the channel back.]

JESSICA: Bob, it makes me feel disrespected when I make a request and you just roll right over me.

BOB: [Silence, more channel surfing.] What?

JESSICA: Bob, would you please change the channel back?

Bob ignores her. Jessica walks out of the room.

> **MANHANDLING MANEUVER:**
>
> 1. Don't say anything else. Just get up and leave the room.
> 2. He'll figure out what he did, come after you, and apologize.
> 3. When he does, thank him for it, give him a kiss, and then enjoy your chick-flick programming.
> 4. If he doesn't respond, do something else until he comes and finds you.
> 5. Your absence will register and he will most likely apologize for being selfish.

When you make a request, don't fight about it. Show your man through your actions that you dislike his behavior and that you won't stick around for it. We have much better things to do with our time, like reading *InStyle* magazine in the bathtub.

Romantic Rule: We don't compromise our dignity or become doormats when we use the three-sentence rule. It's one, two, three strikes, he's OUT.

Conversing with the Emotional Bird

Always be a woman of few words when you need to discipline a man.

Example:

JESSICA: Bob, I don't want to go to the camping fiesta in the woods again this summer.

BOB: WHY NOT? I just bought a new pup tent and I swear it won't rain this year!

JESSICA: Bob, I just don't feel comfortable going. Thank you, but no.

BOB: Dammit! Why don't you want to go? Come on, don't be a spoilsport! What, you can't take a little rain, and mud? [Slams fridge door, stomps around the room.]

JESSICA: Bob, I don't want to fight about it. I just don't want to. Okay, I am going to take the dog for a walk now.

WARNING: Time to get out of Dodge.

When you come back, restate your concern: "I'm sorry you're disappointed, but I really want to talk about going to Venice together, like we agreed we would last year." When he complies, use the rewards system of man management and stroke him.

MANHANDLING MANEUVER: Never prepare men for big talks. Just ambush them when they're in a pleasant mood and state your case in three sentences, tops. Don't get M.A.D.D., get even!

"No" Is a Complete Sentence

If your man pushes you to do something you don't want to do, just say no. You don't have to explain it. Just claim it and state it. The less you say, the stronger your position will be. Reason: Women often feel guilty when they say no. We tend to over explain why we can't do something in an effort to not hurt other people's feelings.

Men, however, will often use your explanation as ammunition and try to pick apart your case and break down your defenses by finding the loophole in your logic. This is what they do at work. And this strategy usually works on girlfriends.

So just say, *"No!"* and stand there. He will have absolutely nowhere to go. And then he'll ask, "Why not?"

YOU: It's just my gut feeling. This is just not sitting right with me.

Remember, no one can ever tell you that your gut feeling is wrong. Most people recognize that *"the still, small voice inside of you"* is holy ground, often God-inspired, and most men are wise enough to stop arguing once this statement's been uttered. They'll back away from your hot topic and look at you as one possessed by spirits.

Boo!

Don't Corner Your Man
"Three Strikes You're Out & The Three Sentence Rule

When a man is upset or irritated, it is only common sense to wait until he's smoothed out his feathers before trying to make him speak on command (i.e. engaging him in a *"relationship talk"*). If you persist in trying to make him perform this trick, you're only liable to hear some very unpleasant screeching, and your prodding will provoke aggression, pecking, sneering, or other hostile behavior.

He needs to be put back in the cage for a relationship time-out, until he settles down.

The best way to defuse the situation is to say, "Hon, you seem upset right now. Why don't we take a break and talk about this later when you're calmer?"

MAN FACT: *When men are irritated, don't back them into a corner by making them speak on command, or they'll attack!*

How to Train a Screamer

No one deserves to be screamed at . . . not (even) men and most certainly not you! If you have a screamer on your hands, the bad news is that he's going to be a total pain, but the good news is that retraining him is a possibility, if, and only if, you use the following training routine religiously . .. and have very thick skin.

MANHANDLING MANEUVER: *You must commit to gaining the upper hand. You must set a boundary with him every single time that he starts to act up. If he won't take correction and pipe down, you must immediately leave the house, the restaurant, or the relationship, to teach this loudmouth that you won't put up with his negative behavior.*

Tip: Screamers are screamers because they like to scream. It works for them and is an effective tactic that they use to make things go their way. It's not your fault that he's screeching at you, so don't take it personally. Never engage in a screaming match unless you like yelling, too.

Shut Him Up or Shut Him Down

The following technique is taught in self-defense classes to thwart would-be attackers. Here's how to beat Old Yeller at his noisy game.

As soon as he starts to shout, put your hands up like Miss Diana Ross and say, "STOP!" once, and very firmly. This will stun him. He may act like he flew right into a plate glass window and stop dead in his tracks. He may even take a step or two back.

Then say, "You may not speak to me in that tone of voice." And stare him down. If he pipes right up again, repeat the same gesture and give the next verbal command: "Stop. Do not raise your voice to me!" *(Try practicing this process several times in the mirror or with girlfriends.)* If he refuses to knock it off and is unable to contain himself, say, "You are too angry right now. We will talk when you are calmer." Turn on your heel and then silently and swiftly leave the room.

If he screams down the hall after you, do not speak to him or re-ward this behavior by giving him any more of your precious attention. Quickly leave the scene. He has lost the privilege of communicating with you for the time being. Stick to it! Create a complete No Access Zone around you, which includes cell phones, texting, social media un-friending, and e-mails, too.

Your Big Squawker will soon learn that you won't stand for his unacceptable behavior and he'll gradually knock it off because it fails to work on you. You'll successfully set a new standard of behavior for him and he'll be a keeper, not a screecher.

WARNING : If you are inconsistent with this training, he won't believe you or respect you, and the next time you try it, he'll remain an incorrigible loudmouth.

You deserve better. So stick to it. You're worth it!

MANHANDLING MANEUVER: *Don't stick around for bad behavior. Quickly Cover the Cage and give him a time-out.*

Feather-Picking (on You)

This bad habit is caused by boredom and pent-up energy. If your naughty bird starts picking on you, quickly nip it in the bud. Never, ever allow a man to ridicule you. To shut him up, say, "You're entitled to your opinion, but I don't have to listen to it. It's hurtful." Then Cover the Cage by leaving the room or hanging up the phone . . . and then why not pull out your little black book and take a look? Or take up boxing and start practicing a great left hook!

Magic Words
How to Spot Fighting With Your Man

If you've tried everything else and nothing seems to work, you can always resort to magic. The following words are to be used only in a last-ditch effort to save your sanity. They are guaranteed to make a Trumpeter Swan as quiet as a House Wren.

Reciting these spells will allow for a little relationship cooldown period and give you the upper hand. In the heat of any argument, simply say, *"You might be right, Dwight,"* or *"All right, Zack, let me think about that!"*

Don't say anything more. Let him sputter around for a minute and wind down. You may have to repeat these sentences several times to reassure him that the fight is really over (for now) to complete his transformation from noisy and peckish to refreshingly mute.

But if he still won't pipe down, try, "Would a blow job make you shut your trap?" and I guarantee that he'll pipe down in two seconds flat!

twenty-eight

Peckerheads

Healthy men find it natural to want to make women happy. They protect and care for females, children, and society at large, instinctively. These noble birds don't worry too much about themselves because they know that when they provide care for others, their needs will be automatically taken care of, too.

So, when Average Joe's ante up, they begin to possess a measure of greatness, enough to become heroic in the bedroom, in the boardroom, or on the battlefield. And we salute them! Because your happiness is the key to his sense of self-esteem, your ongoing love, trust, and respect will surely be his reward.

(Unless you're psycho.)

Then there are Peckerheads. These men are more like large boys zipped into man-suits. The Peckerhead is selfish, self-involved, and under the mistaken impression that women, relationships, and the entire world at large are simply there for his pleasure. He will deforest a nature preserve and quickly strip mine your heart. He is conscience-free and won't adapt his hurtful or selfish behavior to accommodate your needs. Why should he? Your happiness doesn't come first. His does! No matter how charming he appears to be at first glance, you'll soon learn that the pecking order of this relationship puts your needs at the bottom, and his right on top, where, I might add, he can take perfect aim!

Romantic Rule: How you and your partner deal with troubles, trials, and tribulations will be a source of renewed camaraderie and understanding or divisive and destructive battling. So choose well, my lady.

When His Feathers Are Ruffled:
How to Spot the Problem Male

You wouldn't want to handle an angry or aggressive bird without put-ting protective gear on first. Ergo, when a man is angry or upset, it's always wise to handle him with kid gloves.

Now, if your bird is chronically upset, irritable, and angry, it begs the obvious question of what in God's name you're still doing with him. Life's too short to be tyrannized by a badly behaved man. You must be able to retrain him. If he cannot be easily domesticated, quickly release him back into the wild before he destroys your peace of mind (or your furniture).

Most often, when men are upset, they take off in various Flight Patterns, as we've previously discussed. They flee your presence and then alight on your perch once they're delight-fully human again. Other males, however, don't leave the cage, and will actually bar the door and fight it out with you. This oc-curs when a conflict triggers his *Fight Pattern.* In this case, men draw their swords and are willing to duel. A sparring match with an angry Raptor is unpleasant. He's lost all sight of you and has gone into battle mode and is rattling his rusty sword.

Warning Signs
He may start picking on you, taunting you, or even become meaner when you start to cry. When men do this, you must put them into total isolation because the man you love has just morphed.

The man you love has turned into a . . .

Peckerhead. This condition occurs when your tears make him feel manipulated and he actually becomes meaner if he's made you cry. Or he's feeling guilty about something and won't cop to his bad behavior, so he'll start a fight to alleviate his guilt and make himself feel better. This is a terrible state of affairs and should not be allowed to continue. It should be a temporary condition and exhibited on rare occasions. If this happens more than twice a year, you have misdiagnosed this condition. You have confused the garden-variety Peckerhead with a . . .

Toxic Peckerhead. This man just likes to fight. Men who like to fight do it to find relief from their own crappy and stressful feelings. Toxic Peckerheads pick fights with valet parking attendants, ticket takers, total strangers, and their girlfriends. This is their version of stress management. Toxic Peckerheads are incapable of blissful domestication or loving pair bonding. They repeatedly betray your goodwill and your relationship by recurrent screaming, nipping, and nit-picking. They'll often blame their bad behavior on you. Don't fall for it! This bad bird is a big bully and wants a (smaller) sparring partner to use as an emotional punching bag for his do-it-at-home anger-management workout.

Early "warring" signs: He has road rage. He often yells when he reenacts hostile confrontations that he's had with someone else, and often while you're both stuck in the car. The tip-off to his aggressive behavior may come early in your relationship, but you may disregard it because it has nothing to do with you (yet!). But soon, you'll see it directed at you.

QUESTION: *Do you really want to climb into the cockfighting ring with him? Will your manicure survive?*

WARNING: *If you're trying to housebreak a Toxic Peckerhead, don't do it alone. Call a therapist for an intervention. Or save yourself the drama and just call the movers instead.*

Does He Turn a Deaf Ear
To Your Distress Call?

I was at a cocktail party one night when I spied some interesting relationship behavior between Maggie, a brilliant colleague of mine, and her husband, Jimmy. He would peer around a corner, spot Maggie, and then give her a thumbs-up sign, and once she returned it, dash off again.

"Maggie," I asked, "what's up with Jimmy? He's acting kind of funny."

"Oh, the last time we went to a party he ignored me all night, and when I told him about it, it must've made an impression. He's just making sure I'm all right." She giggled. "I love that Jimmy!"

Observation: Maggie told her husband how she felt; Jimmy listened to her sadness and came up with an adorable solution. Getting her needs met by Jimmy is easy because he is not a peckerhead.

But what happens if you're with someone who responds like Clark?

The Switcharoo

"Clark, it really bothered me when you left me alone at the party last night. I felt kind of left out. You didn't seem to notice that you weren't including me in conversation."

"Jesus, will you get off my back? Why are you so sensitive/needy/clingy/insecure?!"

Clark just turned your valid need into an insult. He's a Peckerhead! Or how about Matt . . .

The Swoop and Kill

You: "Matt, it really bothered me when you left me alone at the party last night. It made me feel left out."

Matt: "Fine. Next time I'll just go by myself if you hate my friends so much!"

Matt dismissed your need entirely and trumped it with a threat or punishment. He's a big bully!

And what happens when we discuss our tender feelings with Jack?

Big Baby with a Broken Wing

> You: "Jack, it really upset me when you left me alone at the party last night. Your weird friend kept hitting on me."
> Jack: "Would you stop busting my balls? I have a horrible headache. All you ever do is complain. I can't do anything right! Where's the Advil?"

Jack avoids the issue and acts like the victim, *instead*. He's a manipulative baby!

Tip: Men who think you're busting their balls when you make sincere requests are *out of order*. They are defending their right to be unworkable and unchangeable. Women are very susceptible to big babies because we hate to think we're hurting *anyone*, even men who are perfectly okay with *hurting us*.

Romantic Rule: *Men need to take your coaching without acting like they're getting their balls busted.*

Self-Exam: Is It PMS or Is It Him?

Sometimes Peckerheads try to convince you that you're totally nuts for feeling upset. They dismiss your request by calling you crazy, too sensitive to live, or PMS'd!

The Kid Glove Test: If a friend called and told you the exact same story, would you think she had a good reason for being upset or angry? Or would you think she was overreacting, creating drama, and that her boyfriend actually had a valid point?

(But I'm on your side, and it's probably/definitely HIM.)

The Fighting Cock

Fighting Cocks are dangerous birds of the wild. It may be disastrous to remove them from their natural habitats (inner rings of Hades) to try and tame them.

The Fighting Cock is also known as the I'm-Not-Going-to-Jump-Through-Hoops-for-You Guy. He is so insecure that even asking him to consider your feelings will be perceived as an affront to his masculinity. He'll quickly dig in his heels and obstinately refuse to cooperate for pleasant indoor living.

Fighting Cocks suffer from Little Dick Syndrome and try to boost their low self-esteem by fighting with women (and total strangers). Your needs are a perfect place for the assault because it's where you're already feeling vulnerable. Once you make a request, no matter how small or heartfelt, a Fighting Cock will throw down the gauntlet and refuse to cooperate with you as a personal point of honor. He childishly behaves like it's beneath his dignity to care about your feelings or to change his behavior for you in the slightest. He doesn't care about making you happy. He hates himself so much that he wants you to be unhappy, too. His is a dangerous kingdom, ruled by a crazy king.

Thank God he doesn't have a guillotine!

Romantic Rule: *Don't try and partner with men who are chronically oppositional and refuse to compromise. Even if they are celebrities!*

The Fighting Cock thinks women are there to please him, no matter how badly he treats them.

If you have this foul fowl on your hands, get out the chopping block, preheat oven to 350 degrees, and make a tasty dead duck l'orange!

MAN FACT: *Hygiene issues are correctable with a good bar of soap, but a poor character is not so easily remedied!*

How to Spot the Difference Between "The Noble Bird" & "A Peckerhead"

If he . . .

- is a graceful loser

- respects your boundaries

- recovers quickly from discord

- doesn't carry a grudge

- fights fair

- compromises

- takes responsibility for his part

He's a Noble Bird!

But if . . .

- he blames you, refuses to apologize, and punishes you

- his inner sense of self-worth depends on winning every argument

- he turns on you or tries to bully you, then . . .

. . . He's a Peckerhead.

WTF? Do I Have to Act Like a Saint?

By now, you may have realized that it will take the patience of a saint to handle the little crappers. When you're at your wits' end, try the Saint Francis prayer. He is the patron saint of all women desperately trying not to break several clauses listed in the Ten Commandments when dealing with the most maddening of all of God's creatures next to horseflies, men.

Saint Francis was famous for three interesting things:
1. He meditated for hours in the woods.
2. He meditated for hours in the woods, in the nude.
3. He was so relaxed, birds perched on him!

Whenever you need an attitude adjustment of your own, shut the door, grab a magazine, lock the door, and give Saint Francis a shot before committing relationship homicide.

Or you can try this shorthand version: *"Dear God!! Don't let me fricassee my boyfriend!"*

Post It Note

Everyone has idiosyncrasies and quirks. They're a part of the eccentric charm of being you. You need a man who doesn't think that you're too much work . . . for him. And vice versa. The right guy will turn your fear of bats into an opportunity for him to show his love by escorting you safely out of a dark, smelly bat-ridden cave.

Translation: Your hero!

twenty-nine

Putting All of Your Eggs in One Basket

Most men will delay moving the relationship forward, even if they're madly in love with you, because they innately fear emotional lock down. Unless you're dealing with a Homing Pigeon, you'll have to remind them when the expiration date on their exclusivity freebie is up. If, as the date approaches, your bird still hasn't said a peep about it, you should alert him thusly: *"Jackson, we've been dating for almost one year. I won't feel comfortable continuing our relationship without an engagement, as we have discussed before."*

Then stop talking and hear him out. If he has a wonderful surprise for you, magnifique!! But if your boyfriend is like most men, he'll just try to duck the question to buy himself more time, test your resolve, and try to maintain the status quo. This is your cue to put on your badge and lay down the law: say, *"I love you babe, but if you don't want to move forward, I will need to move on."*

Now watch, wait, and listen . . .

At this juncture, most birds usually start singing a very long list of excuses to prevent their permanent capture. Don't become alarmed if they pitch a fit, pick weird fights, become cold and withdrawn, or even threaten to end the relationship. He'll try very hard to regain control, and do everything in his power to make you extend the deadline, and duck your request, by terrorizing you.

The Duck and Cover

The art of avoidance, evasion, and lying (by omission) is a basic survival tactic that your Lovebird will exhibit to greater or lesser degrees when confronted with the prospect of having *"the talk."* This tactic is the hands-down favorite go-to strategy that men use anytime a hot topic comes up that they don't want to discuss. Men employ the art of avoidance to ensure that your agenda won't ever come up for discussion.

Romantic Rule: Conversations about important topics are commitments!

If you have "the talk," he'll be forced to take a stand. Otherwise, a man continues to reap the benefits of all the "free stuff" he's been getting without having to make a deeper commitment. Let's take a look at how men masterfully resist emotional arrest by keeping your relationship in a holding pattern, so they can stay Top Bird and keep calling the shots.

Tactic 1: Avoidance

AVOIDANCE: n 1. deliberately avoiding; keeping away from or preventing from happening. 2. *"Babe, I'm already late for work . . . can we talk about this later? Gotta run!"*

Avoidance by stalling and delaying the danger.

You: "Where is this relationship going? When can we talk about getting married?"
Him: "Can we talk about this later? I can't even think about that right now. I have to [finish my dissertation, get a promotion, buy a house, get my ex to sign the divorce papers, pay off my student loan, win that trip to the Caribbean, climb Mount Kilimanjaro before I can even think about being ready to discuss that! Okay? Will you pass me the chips?"

Avoidance by feigning illness. He may suddenly get a headache, backache, or some other impossible to prove he's just faking it to avoid having a serious conversation type of ailment: "I have a really bad headache right now. Can we talk about this later? Would you rub my back a sec . . . ahhh, that feels so good!"

Avoidance by flying out of the room.

He manages to disappear right in the middle of the conversation. He may wander out of the room, start another activity, or suddenly remember he needs to go to work, run an errand, or return to his apartment, thus masterfully managing to escape having "the talk."

Tactic 2: Evasion

EVASION *n* 1. a statement that isn't literally false but that cleverly avoids an unpleasant truth. 2. the act of physically escaping from something (an opponent or a pursuer or an unpleasant situation) by some adroit maneuver. *"Hey, hon, I'm gonna make a beer run. Back in a few!"*

MAN FACT: *Men know that withdrawing their attention drives women crazy. Your bird may actively choose to pull his attention away to punish you for trying to have "the talk," to get you right where he wants you—on the branch below him, and out of your tree!*

You start to have "The Talk," but he changes the subject by bullying you. He gets really mean, upset, or grumpy to throw you off balance and scare you out of having "The Talk." *"You have such crappy timing! If you need an answer right now, then the answer is NO! Why do you always do this? Can't we just have a good time? This is the last time I ever take you on vacation. Jesus!"*

Tactic 3: The Boomerang

He derails the conversation by talking about some beef that he has with you instead. He plays a verbal shell game called "the Boomerang." It's very easy to get knocked off balance by this maneuver until you understand it. This is how it works.

YOU: Moe, I've been patient, but now that your divorce is finalized, I'd like to discuss when we are going to get married.

MOE: You have got to be kidding me. I'm still steamed about what happened yesterday at the barbecue. Why did you wear such a low cut blouse to my mother's house?

Respond thusly: "You're changing the subject. We can discuss my wardrobe, but not until you answer my question."

Then restate your topic again. See if it gets any traction . . . or if it goes straight to hell in a hand basket like this . . .

YOU: Moe, it's been four years now and I've been really patient. You said we would discuss this after your divorce was finalized, and it is.

MOE: If you aren't happy with the way things are right now, then why should I marry you? I don't want to be with someone who's unhappy.

YOU: Well, I am happy, but I'm not happy with the status of our relationship, especially after we came up with a date together . . . and that date has come and gone.

MOE: Well, I obviously can't make you happy, so let's not discuss marriage. Happiness should build on happiness. I'm not going to jump through hoops trying to please someone who can't be happy right now!

Okay, this man's doing flips than Nemo in *The Matrix.* an attempt to keep you spinning and knock you off balance. If you're engaged in a conversation with a man who tries this maneuver, the only thing to do is to stand up for yourself. Be prepared to walk . . . or submit to his terms and "Kiss The Ring." (Homework: Watch The Godfather. parts 1, 2 & 3)

WARNING: Savvy Romantic Researchers don't fall for avoidance routines, even when these excuses sound plausible. You've got him on the run!

When men start exhibiting "avoidant behavior" (and start flying around in a panic), it's actually a very good sign. Enjoy their flighty display! They're taking you *seriously*. They now know that you're no longer willing to "wing it" anymore, and are climbing out of the "No-Time-Frame Dating" trap! You were clear about your "test drive" time-frame, and no he'll need to honor it, in order to keep you.

So always remember: If he says that the *"timing just isn't right"* or that your relationship isn't *"perfect enough yet,"* remember this . . .

Romantic Rule: Marriage vows are "For better or for worse," not "For better and completely perfect."

Does Your Relationship Add Up?

Let's do an assessment of your fieldwork and examine what's wound up in your nest. Once you learn a bit of relationship math, you can save yourself years of heartache—and its ultimate result: division! Use this romantic calculus to quickly predict your relationship's probable outcome.

Bad Math: 1 + 1 =1

Two incomplete and wounded people cling to one another in an attempt to make one whole person. This is the *"you and me against the world, babe"* relationship, which is codependent in nature. One or both partners may be in *"active"* addiction or have poor boundaries from growing up in a dysfunctional family. The hallmark of this relationship is that one or both partners feel like they've taken on too much responsibility for the well-being of the other, as if they've been taken an emotional hostages which creates an unhealthy and immature relationship paradigm.

Relationship Calculation = You're LOONS

Romantic Division:
1 +1= 0

Two individuals are complete in and of themselves, but they don't know how to compromise, surrender, or sacrifice their personal agendas for the good of the relationship. One or the both of them acts like the relationship is there only to serve them, and this selfishness will be their undoing. Partners fight tooth and nail to get their way and don't see the real damage they're inflicting on their mate. The hallmark of this relationship is intense power struggles and ceaseless fighting. This couple's inability to compromise and problem solve will eventually undermine any peace or happiness they once had. They may leave the relationship as bitter enemies.

Relationship Calculation = The COCKFIGHTING DUO

Romantic Multiplication:
1 +1 = 3

This is the ideal partnership equation. You are separate but whole individuals, and you've come together to form a third entity: your relationship. You learn how to balance your individual needs with the needs of the relationship. You know how to problem solve with each other respectfully and fairly. You are in a mutually responsible and loving partnership that can span the ages of time.

Relationship Calculation = You're LOVEBIRDS!

thirty

Swan Songs

Delivering the Timely Ultimatum

The following maneuver should only be used if you're committed to your personal relationship goals enough to move on.

How to Get a Man to Step Up or Step Off
Step 1. Cock the Gun

Speak these words only if you're prepared to walk: away and possibly never see him again. Or wind up married to him!

Love Script for The Swan Song

YOU: I can't stay in this relationship if we can't move forward together and make plans for the future. I love you, but I am leaving you. If you ever want the things that I want, I am sure you will let me know. But until then, this relationship is over.

MOE :(Gulp.) Whaaaa?

Step 2. Kick Him Out of the Nest

Immediately break up with him! If you're living together, pack your bags and rent a U-Haul. (Tip: Ask sexy men friends to help you move your furniture! Remember), when you step back, you'll give him room to step up—or step off and stop wasting your time! You deserve a man who loves you enough to honor his word and keep his commitments.

Step 3. Create a Psychic "No-Fly Zone"

If your man stubbornly insists on behaving like a chicken, and stupidly lets you leave him, he may suddenly *"come to"* and try to woo you back with wheelbarrows of flowers, frantic phone calls, and desperate text messages—or the surprise 3 a.m.. tearful drive-by.

WARNING: Don't become flustered and just cave in! He's counting on this kind of over-the-top wooing to get you back in line. Don't see him unless you're sure he means business. Here's how to flush out the truth of his intentions.

The Timely Retreat" *Love Script:* "

Say: "I love you and am sad that you don't want to *(get engaged, have a baby, marry me, move in together, buy a home, have a future with me, etc.)* " I accept your decision. This is very hard for me, so please don't contact me for three months. I'll need some space and the room to move on. Bye, baby."

Now completely stop talking and listen! If he has changed his tune, and says he's ready to step up . . . wunderbar! But if he's still flapping around, he was just testing you. This love script will let him know that you mean business.

Then grab your things and leave, or get off the phone. And stick to your guns! Give him a real time-out, because he actually needs one. He needs time to carefully weigh his options. Does he want to have (a) sex with a slutty stranger in an elevator, or (b) a family, home, children, pets and plants, and someone who'll give a crap when he has a heart attack.

Step 4. The Standoff

Men at this point will try to test your resolve. They'll often fall silent and sullen, and withdraw. Or they'll try to fight it out, in an attempt to get you to "give in" and change your mind. Do Not Fall For This! Until he stops singing *"Freebird"* and starts humming *"Going to the Chapel"* it's TIME. Just pack your bags and walk. *Tip: Wear something ass-tastick or a low cut top!*

During a negotiation, the person who WINS is the person that's willing to walk.

The person who is willing to leave an unworkable situation always has the most leverage and power. So don't give yours up. , buttercup! He must understand that you aren't going to give up on your life goals, and that this is *not a ploy*.

Beware: If you abandon yourself, cave in, and allow yourself to be cajoled without a deeper commitment. Don't return to the status quo.

> **MANHANDLING MANEUVER:** *Don't reward men who are ambivalent about stepping up by continuing to talk to them, date them, or sleep with them!*

Step 5. The Bargaining Phase

He may try to stall for time by saying that he wants to (get engaged, have a baby, marry you, move in together, buy a home, have a future), but not this very second, and make seductive pleas like *"Baby, you'll get everything you want if you just hang in there!"* and *"Relax! We're on the marriage track."* Allow this to fall on deaf ears.

The Secret Male Language Decoder: At this point, the words "maybe" and "hang in there" mean "No!"

Tip: Cover the Cage! No calls, emails, or texts!

Step 6. Let Him Brood

The next three months will be agonizing but well worth the pain and trouble. Suck it up, sister! Shut him down. (Cry all about town, and have hot rebound sex if you wish. It's delish!) Keep your commitment to yourself and leave him in the dust. This is often the only way to stimulate the feeling (courage that most males need to voluntarily fly into the relationship cage and nest with you. Hopefully, your departure will engender the following responses in him: grief, misery, craziness, loss of appetite, tearing of hair, inability to sleep, and feeling like he's been thrown into a pit of despair.

If you're patient, he may wind up crying on your doorstep at three am. with an actual proposal. And a ring!

AMAZING MAN FACT: You can't lose either way! If he flies south, he was just holding up traffic and you've wisely set yourself free to find a true Lovebird. (You've just killed two birds with one stone!) But if he comes back with his hand on his heart, and is ready to pledge allegiance to your flag, you'll be well rewarded. You'll have self-esteem, and a now happy-to-step-up kind of man!

Romantic Result: The eagle has landed!

The Phoenix

Now sometimes fate takes a strange turn. Women with high self-esteem, (after leaving crappy relationships) become free and clear . They are ready to t create serious "Man Magic." And it often waltzes right into your life in two surprising ways.

The Surprising Sequel!   The man who flew south, the same one you *were sure was gone for good,* suddenly pops right back into your life! You never saw it coming, but there he is on the other end of the line, or on your doorstep, or at your college reunion, and he still looks hot! *Ohmygod.*

He confesses that he's missed you after all these (hours, days, weeks, months, or YEARS—whenever you gave him the boot), and he swears that he's finally grown up. He's ready to step up, and begs you to give him one more try . . . and then he kisses you. And he just positively insists that you do!

You don't need my advice about how to handle this rare bird. You can probably figure this one out all by yourself He's stopped being Chicken (or a Bat Out Of Hell) and has into turned into **The Bluebird of Happiness**. And by the way . . . congratulations! Feel free to send me an invite to the wedding! I probably won't be able to make it, but I promise to send you *an absolutely lovely* card!

Tip: Phoenix's are like unicorns. They're magical! But don't hold your breath. They only appear once our heroine's has thoroughly "given up the ghost" and completely moved on.
(*See:Brigitte Jones's Diary* – parts 1 & 2, and every novel by Jane Austin.)

But if you're currently single and want to find your love-bird, he's probably through . . .

Door Number Two!

It's time to go and find lovebirds and start dating anew. As a *Romantic Researcher* you'll discover something surprising. You're a Phoenix, too!

With *Dating, Mating and Manhandling* under your garter belt:

1. You'll start enjoying dating with a new kind of confidence and higher self-esteem.

2. You'll stop dating Wing-nuts, and commit to finding the man of your dreams.

3. You'll get flocked with suitors and find the right man, who's just gob-smacked by you.

'Cause he's out there, I promise.

He's just waiting for you!

The Aviary

appendix: an index of bird types

This helpful Birding Guide will help you identify the bachelors winging around in Cyberspace. Once you decide who your **Target Birds** are, and can spot them with ease, you'll stop confusing rabid avifauna with the wonderful men that are in full view!

The Albatross

This divorced dad has a brood and an angry ex hanging around his neck. And now he's hanging on to yours for dear life!
Warning: If he hates his ex, it'll be like going into a war-torn country and trying to stage a love-in. You'll get undermined and probably nuked.

Habitats: Soccer practice, Toys 'R' Us, school plays, family therapy, Match.com, and Tinder!

Song: "All By Myself"

Plumage: Khakis, Hawaiian shirts, and terrible lace-up shoes, all a-jumble in the closet of his crappy rental apartment. The Ex got the house.

Mating Habits: Desperate. Needy, grabby. May cry before, during, or after sex. *Beware:* Hot dates often get derailed by little people, so bring a turtleneck!

Care and Feeding Tips: Bring Kleenex and practice sympathetic phrases like "Umm-hmm, how awful. There, there." You won't even need to wax to perk him up 'cause his ex refused to have sex with him years ago and he's all backed up.

The Arctic Tern

This is one bird who is never defrosting. Something trau-matic must have happened at boarding school or in foster care. The man's in total emotional lock-down.

Habitats: Uptown, downtown, all around the town.

Song: "Cold as Ice"

Plumage: Brooks Brothers shirts or an orange jumpsuit. May have roman numerals after his name on business card, or his rap sheet.

Mating Habits: Has his secretary (or parole officer) sched-ule dates for him. Tip: Wear a muffler!

The Bald-headed Eagle

This classic May/December romance with Svengali is per-fect for a perky Lolita who needs a little therapy (well, maybe a lot of therapy, but I'm not judging).

Habitats: College campus, college bars, strip clubs... jail!

Song: "Thank Heaven for Little Girls"

Markings: Bald. Says embarrassing things in front of your friends, like *"I'm ready to rock the house"* and *"That band is SO dope!"*

Mating Habits: Bossy, controlling, and pervy, in a very good or completely pathetic kind of way.

Care and Feeding Tips: Slip into your Catholic schoolgirl uniform and Mary Jane's. Warning: Avoid the ex-wife. She'll be about as happy to see you as crow's-feet.

The Bat Out of Hell

Irresistible to anyone who's ever ovulated, this charismatic sex genius has so many exes' names tattooed on him, he's running out of room! This devastatingly handsome bad boy is hot and he knows it.

Habitats: Dark recording studios, tour bus, strip clubs, your knickers.

Song: "I Want You to Want Me"

Markings: Sexual atheism.

Mating Habits: Anything that will put you over the edge.

Care and Feeding: This species soars over open country in search of its main source of entertainment: groupie girls. So hit your knees and give him what he wants—applause, applause, applause. Good night, Cleveland!

The Bird of Paradise

This hot vacation romance is the adult version of the summer love you had at fourteen when tongue kissing was still *totally gross!* He's too hot for you and you both know it. *tip:* Hide your purse.

Habitats: Not America! Cabanas, Club Med vacations, ancient ruins, gazebos, turrets.

Song: You never heard it before, can't understand a word of it, but it's soooo catchy.

Markings: Has accent and a tan, smells like foreign tobacco, cocoa butter, and strange exotic spices. Often has unfortunate body odor, but who cares? You can just jump in the hot tub with him!

Mating Habits: Warning: May suddenly propose. Do not succumb! Leave this Bird of Paradise where you found him and when you're done, fly home. Alone!

Care and Feeding Tips: Lie back and enjoy the ride . . . until he steals your heart (and your jewelry).

The Bluebird of Happiness

You'd given up hope of ever finding your prince when all of a sudden, *bam!* Sometimes dreams really do come true!

Habitats: It's a mystery. The Lords of Karma will decide.

Song: "Some Enchanted Evening"

Plumage: Knows how to match his clothing but not in a gay way.

Mating Habits: Sweeps you right off your feet and right into his arms.

Care and Feeding Tips: Something old, something new, something borrowed, something blue.

The Blue Jay

This A-type go-getter is in the market for a luxury car and the right woman to buckle into the passenger seat of he's Hybrid or Beemer. (He can't afford a Tesla . . yet.) Learn how to make the perfect mojito and climb up the corporate ladder with Mr. Wanna B.Zuckerberg

Habitats: Chatting up investors in business class, country clubs, and working "the lobby" of any conference he attends.

Song: "Life in the Fast Lane."

Plumage: Sector dependent. Suit and Tie Guy or Button Down Shirt, Jeans & Conversation Start Sneakers Scent: Hypnotique and Pure Ambition!

Mating Habits: Flashy! Impresses you with bottles of wine that he can't pronounce but orders with confidence, and rosy talk of the future...

Care and Feeding Tips: What might've been a buy at 10 A.M. can be a sell before the closing bell. So beware: He may not hold his position overnight! To be a long-term investment, show him your assets.

The Bushtit*

This man can't make up his mind. He's insatiably drawn to T & A on you (and everyone else). At first, he's a delight, and then an incredible pest. He may suffer from Sexual A.D.D. O.C.D. and have outstanding warrants at the D.M.V.... He's too racy.

Habitats: Bushtits are everywhere.

Song: "Super Freak"

Markings: Don't worry, he'll spot *you*. He could be posing as anything. (Your pool-boy, your Ex, your accountant, your handyman, and aging Hollywood execs).

Mating Habits: Whenever he can get it!

Care and Feeding Tips: Work "the pole" and look the other way in denial, or immediately hire a private dick. Better yet, why not dump the Bushtit, and find a nice private dick you can have all to yourself?

*Sadly, I did not make this bird up! I'm a Ph.DD. and have a (terrible) reputation to maintain. So feel free to Google the Bushtit if you want to. You'll find that you owe me a little apology, but I'll be happy to forgive you.

The Cardinal

He just loves the Lord.

Habitats: Bible study, prayer groups, Amy Grant & Michael W. Smith concerts, and in the aisle testifying!

Song: "Your Own Personal Jesus"

Markings: Rosy glow, everything on him is ironed and creased, and his best friend is Jesus.

Mating Habits: Not until marriage, silly! And then get ready for the missionary position.

Care and Feeding Tips: Don't cuss. *Say, "I love the Lord, too!" "Thank you, Jesus! Amen!"*

The Chicken

This garden-variety commitment-phobe would rather drown in the rain than get back in the barn. That would be a commitment.

Habitats: You're not quite sure because he's flown the coop.

Song: "Freebird"

Markings: Ring-finger amputee.

Mating Habits: Hot 'n' heavy until you ask where your relationship is going. Then have fun watching him run around in circles.

Care and Feeding Tips: Slice up carrots and celery and put on a boiling pot of water. Lure Chicken into the hen house. Slam door!

The Clay Pigeon

This garden variety pest can't take a hint (Buzz off, Buster!) Clay pigeons get shot down in every gin joint in town, and are great at ducking for cover, and just pop again.

Habitats: Blocking the view of the cute boy who's standing right behind him.

Love Song: That annoying jingle that got stuck in your head, and you want to make it STOP.

Plumage: It doesn't matter. You don't like him anyway.

Mating Habits: The Clay Pigeon Standards: "Haven't I met you somewhere before?" and "Come on..Smile."

The Cockatoo

These guys are bona-fide sex symbols, (aka athletes, movie stars, and underwear models.) They need approval, and need to get it *everywhere!* And they do, they most certainly do. Yum.

Habitats: On set, the tour bus, behind the velvet rope.

Plumage: Free designer duds or selections from their own clothing label. Bling and chinchilla and a Hummer, too.

Love Song: "I'm bringin' Sexy Back"

Mating Habits: When he says he's playing nine holes, he doesn't mean golf.

Care and Feeding Tips: Assume the position and worship. Then pop some gum and ask for an autograph. He may make you agree to do a mutual "Sexual Consent" app before he takes his boxers off.

The Condor

He's flying high in the rarefied atmosphere of his exceptional fame, fortune, power, or prestige. Your garden-variety rock star or financial wizard. Warning: You'll have to survive the Dreaded Entourage of exes, kids, publicists, fans, and hot-stone massage therapists while trying to bag this big boy.

Habitats: The offices of his pricey divorce attorney, business manager, or shrink. Actually, you have no damned clue. He could be *anywhere* and his assistants are paid to fib (and cover his tracks).

Song: "Goldfinger"

Markings: Ink on his hands (from signing contracts or autographs), a photo-op smile, and tons of loot to boot.

Mating Habits: He's so used to being taken care of that he may be lazy in the sack... but you'll have tons of fun with the gardener!

Care and Feeding Tips: Surrounds himself with an entourage of "friends on the payroll" so the trick here is to figure out what you have to offer that the rest of the posse doesn't. *Tip:* It probably rhymes with "Snow Job" or "Fanal Kex."

The Coot

He's as old as the hills and estranged from the rightful heirs to his estate and sizable fortune. (*see* Anna Nicole).

Habitats: Early bird special, intensive care, rest homes, but he's on wheels so he could be anywhere. In winter, see large groups of Coots migrating to Florida.

Song: "Knockin' on Heaven's Door"

Markings: Liver spots and a schoolboy grin.

Mating Habits: He can't anymore, so bring a book. You can have him tucked under the covers by 8:00 and be on top of your lover by 8:09.

Care and Feeding Tips: Wear rubber-soled flats and a nurse's out-fit. Put his head between your breasts and wiggle to make him giggle.

The Crowing Cock

It's all he can think about!

Habitats: Internet chat rooms using the handle 9"4U

(He's often delusional too!)

Love Song: "Birthday 'In Da Club'"

Markings: Male.

Care and Feeding: Lie. Say, *"Ohmygod you're huge!"* and *"Of course I came!"*

The Cuckoo Bird

Master of the double message. He makes even the most confident women want to pop out of a clock.

Habitats: At his (other) girlfriend's house.

Love Song: "Hello, Goodbye"

Markings: Wedding-ring tan line.

Mating Habits: He'll What's App you from his Burner Number.

Care and Feeding Tips: Stop caring!

The Dirty Bird

You wondered where all of your panties went! Has an assortment of punishments for bad behavior, none of which you'll want to miss.

Habitats: Ummm. I'll leave it to your imagination!

Song: "Closer" Nine Inch Nails

Plumage: Leather and a whip, or a collar and leash!

Care and Feeding Tips: Say, *"Well hello, Mr. Grey!"* Make sure he takes you shopping FIRST.

The Dodo Bird

This hot jock is good with his tools, but a very poor speller. (Who cares?) When he asks you to hand him the "duck tape," just tell him to take his shirt off and move your furniture around. Looking at him is like taking a little vacation... until he speaks. Well, I guess all good things must come to an end, must come, must come ... ummm ... what was I saying?

Habitats: Home Depot, Fixing something in your house that broke. GED classes for recidivists, and The Gym.

Song: Singing along with Bruno Mars

Plumage: He's always in workout clothes, but you'd prefer to see him naked!

Mating Habits: Says he, *"Wants to be professional and doesn't date his "clients' but I'll make an exception just for you."* Sweet.

Care and Feeding Tips: Say, *"Do you have a condom in your tool-box?"*

The Dove

He's always strapped for cash but you don't give a hoot because he makes you feel like Juliet. The perfect choice for an Alpha Female with her IRAs in order and cash to burn. Or a college girls on an allowance.

Habitats: Your place, (Doves always have roommates).

Love Song: "Maria" West Side Sotry

Plumage: Thrift-shop chic. Bed-head haircut, drives an uber, bike or scooter.

Mating Habits: Love letters, handwritten poems, flowers pulled from the park, and a devilish spark.

Care and Feeding Tips: Remember to feed him! He's hungry.

The Falcon

This fetishist insists on being domesticated through rigorous training. Or vise-versa! Tricky!

Habitats: Insists on kneeling at your feet, or the other way around!

Love Song: That song from 50 Shades of Grey.

Plumage: He has AMAZING leather pants! .

Mating Habits: I don't have enough room for this here.

Care and Feeding Tips: Say, "Hi Mr. Grey!" Or just give him a smack.

The Fledgling

A delicious snack. This fellas your very own "After-school Special" Card him first! #himtoo

Habitats: Loves yoga, rock climbing, mowing your lawn, and gratefully trimming your bushes.

Song: "Mama Told Me (Not To Come)"

Plumage: Man Bun, and has a priapic condition in his underpants.

Mating Habits: He never stops! Just say, *"You've got to go now, my husband will be home any minute."*

Care and Feeding: Feed him Pop-Tarts when you're in in lingerie.

The Harpee Eagle

This powerful bird of prey flies up to 60 mph through dense jungle, then swoops in and carries you off to Des Moines. Now you're planning the wedding and you don't even remember *dating*.

Habitats: He'll come and find YOU. Wherever you are.

Song: "Sign, Sealed, Delivered"

Plumage: Drives a U-Haul, has extra set of keys.

Mating Habits: You'll be taking conversion class before you know it.

Care and Feeding Tips: Be prepared to "come too" in a few (days, weeks or months), so sublet your apartment; don't give up the lease!

The Hawk

He's got a penchant for law and order, so shape up and take orders from Sarge.

Habitats: He likes to hunt. Gun range, the B&D section of the sex shop, Republican conventions, police stations
(on the right side of the desk!), Neighborhood Watch, vigilante groups, and church.

Love Song: "Battle Hymn of the Republic" and "I Love This Bar."

Plumage: Buzz cut, sunburned neck, aviator sunglasses, Cadillac four-door sedan with trunk space for firearms—if it isn't already filled with them.

Mating Habits: Barks orders from his Barcalounger, discusses Fox news alerts with intensity.

Care and Feeding Tips: Keep meat treats and beer on hand and say, "Yes, sir. Would you like another?" and he'll be saluting you in no time!

The Homing Pigeon

Homer will want you to burn your little black book and Hop on Pop. He's ready to roost, so don't be surprised when he hits his knees on your six-month anniversary, which he'll remember, plan for, and remind you about. If you're on the fence, beware! He'll be roosting with another by the time you get your ass into therapy and realize that the only way to work out your fear of commitment is to *make one.*

Habitats: On the prowl at the jewelry store, and on bended knee.

Love Song: "The Wedding March"

Plumage: Just bought his first house and has ample closet space, or widowed and "Bingo!) He's ready again!

Mating Habits: Romantic dinners, and meetings with the preacher.

Care and Feeding Tips: Say, *"Yes."*

The Horned Owl

This brainy nerd may not fit your GQ fantasy, but may be a surprisingly stellar lover in the sack, and rock your nation. He'll give you multiple orgasms, diagram them to explain their inner workings, and warble a post coitus aria for you, too!

Habitats: Lectures on campus, environmental protests, poetry readings, synagogue, bookstores, libraries, and the symphony!

Song: "She Blinded Me with Science"

Plumage: His outfit may be ill-fitting, but his binary code is perfect.

Mating Habits: Caught your eye on a TED TALK, or was it Match—with the only good picture ever taken of him. And talks about things that you'll try hard to remember..

Care and Feeding Tips: Act like you're listening. Say, *"Wow, that is fascinating!" "How does fusion work again? " Or a simple "Ah-mayzing!" I had NO IDEA! That explains everything!"* will do.

The Ivory-Billed Woodpecker

You thought you were happily married, but when you bump into him, he gives you romantic hot-flashes.

Habitats: High school and college reunions and walks down memory lane. If that doesn't work, Google him.

Love Song: Whatever you danced to at prom!

Plumage: Surrounded by the golden glow from your wild child past, and is still wearing your favorite cologne.

Care and Feeding Tips: Reverie. Illicit affairs while you're at home visiting the folks.

Tip: If you're both single, it could be "your time!"

The Jailbird

He's incarcerated but you still love him.

Habitats: Lock-down. Oops!He's out and in your backyard!

Mating Song: "Can you accept a collect call?"

Markings: Prison tats, scars, gunshot wounds, and a body just this side of heaven.

Mating Habits: The prison kiss: hands raised up against the glass. He's also mastered the five-minute conjugal visit. Warning: Don't bring up anal; he'll take it the wrong way.

Care and Feeding Tips: Bake him a cake with a file inside it. Duh!

The Jaybird

This chipper fellow is fantastic in the bedroom but you wouldn't be caught dead with him in public.

Habitats: You were drinking at..wait, what was the name of that bar?

Mating Song: "Whoomp! (There It Is)."

Markings: No tan lines!

Mating Habits: Anytime, anywhere, as long as it's inappropriate.

Care and Feeding Tips: SPF 40 and forget to wear panties!

The Lark

As in: *"I have no idea why I slept with him ... it was just a lark!"*

Habitats: Cancun, Vegas, Daytona Beach, and Miami. Any local nightclub or gym will do.

Mating Song: Trance

Plumage: You were way too drunk and it was way too dark, but he had nice white teeth that left a naughty little mark and his abs were just amazing!

Mating Habits: Fast! Pickup line: *"Do you live around here?" Let me help you stretch out"*

Care and Feeding Tips: You don't remember but it certainly did the trick!

The Loon

What woman hasn't fallen in love *at least once* with a super sexy but utter manic of a man that was fabulous fun for three dates straight, and then plummeted into a depression?

Habitats: Rehab, lock-down, the pharmacy, the sofa. Your bushes.

Mating Song: "Crazy" by Patsy.

Plumage: Wild eyes and a four-day stubble.

Mating Habits: Intense. and dangerously spontaneous. Shows up at your door at 4 A.M. unannounced, either laughing or crying, or crying and laughing.

Care and Feeding Tips: Drive your Loon to the ASPCA, ASAP.

The Lovebird

Will die of loneliness if not kept in pairs! ADORBS.

Habitats: Your High School Sweetheart, Church, Funeral Home, bereavement groups, obituaries, OurTime.com

Mating Song: Says, *"I loved being married!"*

Plumage: Stars in his eyes.

Mating Habits: Wife Number 1, Wife Number 2 . . . then you!

Care and Feeding Tips: Bring a brisket to the Shiva and casserole to the wake.

The Master Cock

He's the ultimate undercover lover!

Habitats: Lakers games, hip-hop functions, and Jacob the jeweler.

Song: "Magic Stick."

Plumage: Anaconda in the boxers. Track suit, Rolex (could be fake), large diamond in left ear, Escalade, Hummer, or Benz, oh my!

Mating Habits: Cristal and weed. Says irresistible things like *"Baby, you're lookin' kinda skinny!"*

Care and Feeding Tips: Wink, and get ready for a work out! *Tip:* Cocoa butter is a girls best friend!

The Mockingbird

When you ask him if you look fat, he says, *"Yes."* Then when you get upset, he says "being too sensitive" and that he was "just joking." Not.

Habitats: Perched on a branch right above you.

Song: "Kim"

Plumage: Scowling from his soul. He's unattractive on the *inside*.

Mating Habits: Premature ejaculator . . . *eww-ww!*

Care and Feeding Tips: Drop him! Start doing affirmations, go to karate, and change your locks. And then pick up a Master Cock to expedite your emotional healing!

POLICE

The Mynah Bird

This was an insignificant love affair and now you can't figure out how to get rid of him.

Habitats: He's "virtually" everywhere - texting, FB-ing, Social Media Stalking, and now he just hit you up on Linked In!

Song: "I Want You to Want Me" Cheap Trick

Plumage: Wears the sweater that you bought him *every day* to show you how much he still cares.

Mating Habits: He's a Cling-on. Unfriend Him!

Care and Feeding Tips: Denying him access actually inspires his desire. He takes rejection fabulously!

The Nightingale

This honey-tongued smooth talker sings your praises but develops a case of permanent laryngitis when it comes to making a commitment, dammit!

Habitats: Your boudoir. And then hers.

Song: "Smooth Operator."

Plumage: Twelve-year-old blended Scotch, multiple exes, a luxury sports car, and you. And then her. And then maybe you again if you fall for him a second time! Please read Secret Male Lemon Law Disclaimer on page 63.

Mating Habits: Has more lines than a Colombian drug lord. Wines you and dines you, and then shines you on . . . until he calls. Again.

Care and Feeding Tips: Denial. *Yours* and then *his!*

The Nuthatch

Beware a man better groomed and prettier than you! You're not quite sure if this guy's a model/actor or just . . . gay. *Tip:* "Bisexual" also just means . . . gay.

Habitats: Jamba Juice, the gym, Armani Exchange, the mirror.

Song: "Beautiful."

Markings: Killer body, and dresses with panache.

Mating Habits: Picks you up at the gym where he can inspect your abs before he strips you butt naked. Smokers need not apply.

Care and Feeding Tips: To find out if he's bi, say, "Who designed those pants? *They're fabulous!*"

The Ostrich

He won't understand why you were so upset when you found his ex-girlfriend's diaphragm in the medicine chest while you were innocently looking for ... his ex-girlfriend's diaphragm. You'll want to hit him on the head with an iron, but even that won't make an impression, and now he'll be unconscious, and you're in relationship jail, don't get put behind bars, too. You're suffered enough!

Habitats: Deep in de-Nile.

Song: "It Wasn't Me"

Markings: Sand in his bed.

Mating Habits: Changing the subject.

Care and Feeding Tips: Make excuses for him. Excellent match for a woman with poor confrontational skills, or a spy . . . then you can both pretend that nothing is happening, *together*.

The Parrot

This one's a lifer. Says whatever you want to hear and has mastered the difficult phrase "Yes, dear."

Habitats: You can leave the cage door open and he won't fly away!

Song: "Someone to Watch over Me"

Plumage: Wedding band.

Mating Habits: However you want it, and whenever you'll let him have it!

Care and Feeding Tips: He's completely trained and won't drink from the carton.

A Partridge in a Pear Tree

A holiday hookup between Thanksgiving and New Year's, or the desperate Valentine's Day date when you were lonely, or tipsy, or both. This is one mercy shag where you feel sorry for the both of you. Or have a fabulous anniversary date!!!

Habitats: Under the mistletoe.

Song: "Santa Baby"

Markings: So not your type, you can't even pretend this has a chance. The romantic spirit is out on the curb the next week, along with the tree.

Mating Habits: Do you really care? I didn't think so!

Care and Feeding Tips: Say, *"Would you like some eggnog? And then "Let's have a snog."*

The Peacock
(Un-gay version of the Nuthatch)

This preening Don Juan needs to have all eyes on him, at all times. His femmy self-involvement is way beyond metro-sexual. He'll tell you how much he spent on his Prada loafers. Always irritatingly well-groomed, he'll eye you over to check out the competition!

Habitats: The chair (dentists, hair dressers, facialists).

Song: "You're So Vain"

Markings: Has more facial products than you, and takes longer to get out of the bathroom. So annoying

Mating Habits: Flashes gorgeous grin and says, *"I love your shoes."* or *"I just did cool sculpt!_*

Care and Feeding Tips: Carry a compact mirror and floss. *Tip: Dress down so you don't upstage him. This Peacock often likes a drab little Wren for a consort.*

The Penguin

He's monogamous, mates for life, and is already dressed for the wedding!

Habitats: Other people's weddings, singles' mixers, speed dating, Match.com.

Song: "All of me" by John Legend

Plumage: Southern drawl or British accent, empty ring finger, tux at the ready, and a bike rack built for two.

Mating Habits: He's fast! Better first-date interrogator than you are. Has the pastor on speed dial. He's a bobsled of love and he wants to go cross-country with you. See Stork.

Care and Feeding Tips: Say, *"I'd be honored to be Mrs. [Whatever his last name is]".* . . . and then make him a highball and rumaki!

The Pigeon

This "rat with wings" keeps crapping all over you.

Habitats: Your ATM card, your couch, your car, and after you kick him out, her ATM, her couch, her car.

Song: "Just a Gigolo."

Plumage: Whatever you bought for him.

Mating Habits: Ask him to shower before 'cause he's dirty!

Care and Feeding Tips: Crumbs! Don't overfeed or he'll definitely take advantage. Tip: Put your valuables in the wall safe.

The Pink Flamingo

The Flamingo monopolizes all of your time, but he's hard to resist because he's The Best Boyfriend Ever! And girlfriend, too!

Habitats: Your mirror, your closet (where you catch him trying to jam his big feet into your designer shoes). Or dancing on the table at The Abbey.

Song: "Covergirl" by Mamma Ru.

Plumage: Anything more expensive than what you're wearing.

Mating Habits: He'll hate your ex as much as you do...and want the make-up sex just as badly! Don't fall in love with him or you so won't be screwed.

Care and Feeding Tips: A fashion crisis, celebrity gossip, and boy trouble. To snag him, say *"Want to watch House-wives" and have a cuddle? Tip: You can paint each other's toes and not have sex!"*

The Raven

Heartbroken and pacing your living room floor,
And completely obsessed with his ex named Lenore,
Save yourself the aggravation, just show him the door.
Your Romantic Prognosis: Nevermore. Nevermore.

The Roadrunner

Comes on hot and heavy, then drops you right where he found you. Ouch.

Habitats: Route 66.

Song: "On the Road Again" and "Freefallin"

Plumage: It's a blur, he moves too fast.

Mating Habits: "Wham, Bam, Thank you, Ma'am!"

Care and Feeding Tips: Leave the door open.

The Robin Redbreast

You just love him, and so do all of his ex-girlfriends, his mother, his yoga instructor, and even you suspect, some of his guy friends ...'cause let's face it, he's Prince Charming.

Plumage: Baseball cap, smile lines, and a tan from doing unforced yard work. He really likes doing chores!

Habitats: The park, the Y, or his mom's kitchen flipping burgers for the whole family.

Song: "Close to You." The Carpenters classic

Mating Habits: Will romance you at barbecues, sports bars, your local park, or on lover's lane after dark.

Care and Feeding Tips: Learn how to share your toys if sweet Robin wants to roost with you. He really is the boy wonder and everybody loves him. But good for you if he falls for you!

The Rubber Ducky

This is one birdie that's made to order!

Habitats: Your nightstand drawer.

Song: "I Touch Myself."

Markings: Comes in a variety of colors and sizes, both plastic and rubber.

Care and Feeding: Triple A's or an extension cord will do. Shake a tail feather, baby!

The Scrub Jay

This adulterous bird is also an unrepentant freeloader. A tremendous appendage and pimp-style mind control.

Habitats: His caddy, the track, the corner.

Song: "Just a gigolo"

Markings: He's always suited and booted in swank Gators, Playa chalice, and bejeweled pimp hand.

Mating Habits: The bitch slap.

Care and Feeding Tips: Just bring him the money, honey!

The Sparrow

Accountants, IT people, dentists and the like. This is not a glamorous bird, but you may accidentally fall deeply in love with his codependent tendencies and your newly balanced checkbook.

Habitats: Online, Tinder, his parents' house, and blind dates . . . everyone always tries to help the Sparrow out because they know he needs an assist. It's a mitzvah!

Song: "My Guy."

Plumage: Prius, Kia or Mini Cooper if he's sporty, Polo shirts, pressed pants, and the all-important pocket protector.

Mating Habits: Sincere and (yawn) boring. But your mother will be delighted. He's reliable!

Care and Feeding Tips: Say, *"Sure. Why not."*

The Stork

The Stork can be the most dangerous bird of 'em all. He has a need to "spread his seed." He'll sidetrack your dreams, your ambition, and your career with one sabotaged condom. Often this is the reformed bachelor in his forties who meets a hot twenty-something and knows that this time, it's the real thing. Again. He's finally ready.

Habitats: Lamaze classes, Planned Parenthood, Babies 'R' Us.

Plumage: Has stroller in the trunk, and more baby mammas than an NBA player.

Song: "God's Country"

Mating Habits: Won't wanna keep his Trojan on.

Care and Feeding Tips: Ovulate.

The Toucan

If he can put it up his bill, he will. This fruit loop is a jet-set party boy!

Habitats: Fashion shows, yachts, Bottega Veneta, the A-List.

Song: "White Lines."

Mating Habits: Says, *"Want a bump?" "Are you a model?"*
Plumage: Maserati, Lambo, and anything really expensive that still looks cheap and shiny.

Care and Feeding Tips: Keep the following in your purse: your passport, a bikini bottom, a razor blade, and a mirror.

The Turkey

The Turkey opens HIS car door first when it's raining or says, "Yes" when you ask if he'd like you to "chip in." He'll even watch you struggle with your luggage! He's often CHEEP and lazy.

Habitats: KFC, drive-thru's, and fine mall dining.

Song: Says, *"Why are you wearing your shoes in bed?"*

Plumage: Belly jelly, stains on shirts, sandals with socks.

Mating Habits: Quotes *The Simpsons*. Dream dates include Sizzler, drive-through s, strange international foods found in strip malls.

Care and Feeding Tips: Fresh batteries for remote or vibrator, because he's way too lazy to entertain you.

The Turtledove

He's so sweet that even though he's allergic to kittens, he's doesn't want to hurt their feelings, so he pets them with mittens!

Habitats: His place. Online with a pseudonym, late-night bookstores, the pharmacy (tends toward hypochondria) or tucked into a quiet corner of the library.

Song: "Creep"

Plumage: Sunglasses, Purell, and cigarettes. When nervous has a cute little stutter.

Mating Habits: You'll have to make the first move, so be prepared to be shot down several times before he consents. He may totally blow your mind in the bedroom, so be patient. He's worth it.

Care and Feeding Tips: Coax him out of his shell and into your bedroom slowly. Tip: No sudden movements. He's easily startled!

The Ugly Duckling

He's *so* not your type, but when you give him a chance, he magically turns into a swan!

Habitats: Whenever and wherever you need him.

Song: "My Funny Valentine."

Markings: Ugly, and then actually quite handsome.

Care and Feeding Tips: A closer look!

The Vampire Bat

This bloodsucker will charm you, but once you're under his spell, he will drain you as dry as the Sahara. This man is into power and needs to diminish yours to feel better about himself. This can range from mere psychological abuse to financial demands or even violence. Save yourself! Eat Italian and grab a crucifix and quickly drive a stake through the relationship's heart. If that doesn't work, call my cousin Tony and ask him to pay the bloodsucker a visit!

Habitats: The dark side.

Song: "Under My Thumb"

Markings: Seductive ways soon give way to foul temper and a permanent scowl.

Mating Habits: This Prince Charming turns into Attila the Hun, and then magically reappears again when your bags are packed.

Care and Feeding Tips: Therapy and a Taser.

The Vulture

He loves dating wounded prey. Puts the moves on you at a funeral, the police station, or a self-help groups. This opportunistic predator has no shame. Beware if he's your therapist!

Habitats: Funerals, police stations, court, cruising self-help groups.

Song: "Soldier" by the Beibs

Plumage: Carries Kleenex, and a bail bondsman's number.

Mating Habits: Says, *"Let me buy you a cup of coffee." "Tell me all about it."*

Care and Feeding Tips: Sniffle. Bring a sob story and the final floursih: Wipe your tears on his hankie.

The White Pelican

Garden variety middle-aged white man.

Habitats: Jazz fests, steak houses, pretending to be on the treadmill, not pedaling a stationary bike, sofa in the TV room, heavy metal reunions.

Song: Classic Rock

Plumage: Belly hanging over his shorts, Teva sandals with socks, Hawaiian shirts, and pasty-white (hairy) legs (yick). Collects BBCs and visors, and wears them, even the embarrassing umbrella hat with beer funnel and thinks you'll find it charming. (It sorta is!)

Mating Habits: "The American Classic" (Dinner and a movie.)

Care and Feeding Tips: Always wants another helping. Help him correctly button up his (rumpled) shirt, and keep Tums handy.

The Wild Turkey

Garden-variety party boy. He just busted out of rehab.

Habitats: The bar, the package store, the floor.

Song: "Margaritaville."

Plumage: A hangover.

Mating Habits: Oh, jeez, just get him off me! He's passed out, mid-flight.

Care and Feeding Tips: You'll be the other woman to the bottle, the coke vial, or the beer can. Tip: The Wild Turkey's probably not for you, unless you love being a barfly, too.

The Woodpecker

He'll rock your nation and make you pledge allegiance to his flag. Fireworks!!

Habitats: The bedroom floor, the bathtub, the kitchen counter, the dining room tabletop, up against the wall in the foyer, the elevator...whoops! We're back in the foyer again . . .

Song: "Pony" by Ginuwine

Plumage: A permanent stiffy, encased in tight underwear (for control).

Mating Habits: Drills the hole anytime, any-place; your neighbors are registering noise complaints. But you don't care. They can get a life!

Care and Feeding Tips: Lube and a towel.

The Wounded Bird

He has more issues than a magazine kiosk. This guy will suck you drier than a bone in the desert and suspect you're the one who needs professional help for *even thinking* that you could rehabilitate him. He has a point!

Habitats: Your shoulder, the self-help section, lying on the train tracks.

Song: "Love Hurts"

Markings: Tear-stained cheeks, empty bottle of Prozac chased by half a bottle of gin.

Mating Habits: Jealous, possessive, needy. Sad. Depressed. Hostile. Take your pick!

Care and Feeding Tips: Feed him something with a backbone.

And hand in hand by the edge of the sand
They danced by the light of the moon,
The moon, The moon,
They danced by the light of the moon.

–"The Owl and the Pussycat"

About the Author

Tools, Free Stuff & RomanticTech Support

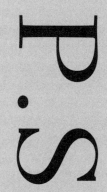

Lauren Frances
Love Coaching

www.Laurenfrances.com
www.Lovescript.com
www.CupidsInbox.com

IG: LaurenfrancesLov
Twitter: LaurensLoveRx
Youtube: LaurensLoveRx

About the Author
Lauren Frances

Lauren Frances is an internationally acclaimed love and relationships expert, bestselling author, speaker, and media personality, and the Founder of Lovscript Bath, Beauty and Boudoir.

Called the "The Doctor of Love" by Extra, "The Flirt Fairy" by Victoria's Secret, and "The Man Whisperer," her unique advice has been featured on numerous TV shows, like The Doctors on NBC, The Real Housewives on Bravo, and on Own, Oxygen, Sky, France 3, Fox, and VH1, and in Elle, Cosmopolitan, Glamour, Self, Star, Redbook, People, Woman's Health, Flaunt magazines, and more.

She penned the The Hollywood Dating Food Chain as a columnist for Flaunt magazine before authoring her internationally acclaimed bestseller, Dating, Mating, and Manhandling - The Ornithological Guide To Men (2006 Harmony Books). Now translated into seven languages, it's been reprinted in trade paperbacks, ebooks and as an audiobook that Lauren also narrated.

Lovescript perfume came as a treat with this edition. To find all of her delicious beauty and bath products, go to www.Lovescript.com.

To find out about Lauren's live events, programs, digital podcasts for online and app dating, and every phase of relating, go to www.LaurenFrances.com!

About Lauren Frances Love Coaching:

Her programs are pure gold! "
-The Sunday Independant

In her private practice, Lauren leads live seminars, live webinars, and digital programs that will show you how to master every relationship phase, from dating, and into deeper partnerships with your lovebird!

Join her **"Romantic Research"** Newsletter for great weekly advice at www.laurenfrances.com

Get her complimentary **Heartache Prevention Podcasts** at: www.CupidsInbox.com!

For Romantic Tech Support, Coaching, and More:

Have a "Love 911" or a Question for Lauren about podcasts, programs, live events or private coaching, or to find out about how to join her **Man Magnet Makeovers, Red Stiletto Tours** to Italy & Paris, and brandspaking new **Boudoir Magnets**, just visit her events page at www.LaurenFrances.com.

And feel free to drop a line at Lauren@laurenfrances.com! And send pics of the ring!